D1716933

THE MASTER ARCHITECT SERIES IV

Ken Woolley

and Ancher Mortlock & Woolley

Selected and Current Works

Ken Woolley

and Ancher Mortlock & Woolley

Selected and Current Works

First published in Australia in 1999 by
The Images Publishing Group Pty Ltd
ACN 059 734 431
6 Bastow Place, Mulgrave, Victoria, 3170
Telephone (61 3) 9561 5544 Facsimile (61 3) 9561 4860

National Library of Australia Cataloguing-in-Publication Data

      Ancher Mortlock and Woolley
      Ken Woolley and Ancher Mortlock & Woolley:
      selected and current works.

      Bibliography.
      Includes index.
      ISBN 1 86470 024 6.

      1. Architects—Australia. 2. Architecture,
      Australian. 3. Architecture, Modern—20th century—Australia.
      I. Woolley, Ken, 1933– II. Title. (Series: Master architect series IV).

  720.994

Edited by Stephen Dobney
Designed by The Graphic Image Studio Pty Ltd,
Mulgrave, Australia
Film by Scanagraphix Australia Pty Ltd
Printed in Hong Kong

Contents

Firm Profile

Preface

By Ken Woolley

There is not much point practising architecture unless it is approached as an art. To do otherwise is to be simply a technical arranger of buildings—a building design professional, maybe, but not one who serves the major need in our cities. Building is the medium of the architect just as paint is the medium of the artist. The public certainly expects the buildings that make up its cities to be more than mere structures—to be artistic, pleasant and beautiful. However, the high cost of a building, compared with that of a painting or a book, imposes important demands on the architect—that the building be functional, durable and economical. To achieve those ends is to earn the right to create the art of architecture in the buildings and should be the essence of the professional practice of architecture.

I have always been interested in understanding what we actually do when we make architecture—how its technical demands and multiple inputs are to be balanced and what attitude should control them. Changes made for the sake of expediency are usually destructive of a building's quality and therefore against the public interest. They need to be resisted if the work is to have any value outside its immediate, albeit important, concerns with function, cost and time. The best way to do this is by referring to similar issues in the other arts, particularly literature, music, painting and sculpture.

I find it interesting that architectural analogies are so often used by musicians to describe their compositions, as though they need to explain the intangible nature of music in terms of the solid form, space and time of experience which characterises architecture. As architects, however, we can benefit from the reverse process by considering music's rhythm and repetition, the occupation of space by sound, the tensions and emotions invoked, the clarity and accuracy of execution, the collaboration of forces to produce the musical work and, finally, the remarkable similarity of the creative prescription: instructions on paper depicting the work and how to perform it—the working drawings, as it were.

It must be obvious that architecture of quality, as demanded by the public, flows from the creative control of its architect. It hardly needs to be argued that careful creative and intuitive choice from available alternatives is the essence of the artistic act. Therefore, any system which puts choices in the hands of others will lead to mere building.

This book sets out to illustrate my work in the context of the practice now known as Ancher Mortlock & Woolley, which was founded by Sydney Ancher in 1945 and later became a partnership with Bryce Mortlock and Stuart Murray. I joined as a partner in 1964 and Ancher retired soon after, followed later by Murray and eventually Mortlock, in 1983. A selection of the work of my colleagues in Ancher Mortlock Murray & Woolley assists in understanding the current status of the firm and the attitude towards excellence which has always driven it. Before joining the firm I had practised for nine years as a design architect in the NSW Government Architect's Branch of the Public Works Department, under Cobden Parkes and then Ted Farmer, my most significant mentor being Harry Rembert, the Assistant Government Architect.

The practice has never set out to be a large corporate structure, but rather to achieve and then maintain a capacity to carry out large-scale works. While it has demonstrated that it can execute several very large projects at one time, its policy has been to restrict its output to the capacity of the established creative team. This has never been a problem, because worthwhile projects are limited in number and have to be vigorously and competitively pursued. Expansion for its own sake inevitably leads to taking on projects with little chance of merit and producing mediocrity.

Instead, the firm has offered special characteristics to its clients: that creative control is focused at principal level; that the firm's directors are the project directors and design managers, not merely administrators; and that clients are not committed to unknown, untried capacities at what is sometimes called "project architect" level.

All architects carrying out major work need to set up management structures and resources capable of handling numerous staff, among whose inputs are the application and development of design ideas which must be controlled by their originator. Such has been the nature of this practice; there must be a collaborative effort, but it must be consistent. Maintaining this balance is one of our challenges for the future.

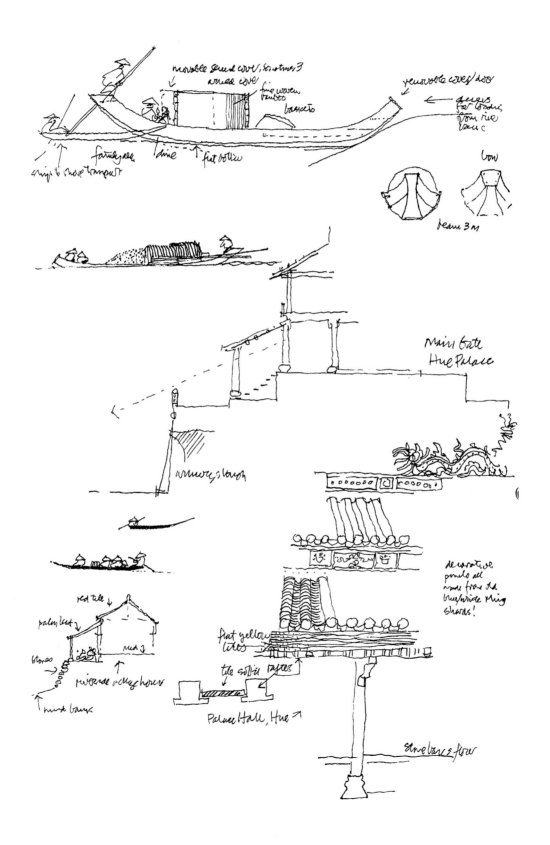

movable grass cover, sometimes 3
arched cove

fine woven bamboo baskets

removable cover/door

designs for loading from river bank

family sail

line

flat bottom

ships to shore transport

bow

beam 3 m

Main Gate
Hue Palace

armourer's lodge

decorative panels all made from old blue/white Ming shards!

red tile

palm leaf

mud

stones

riverside village houses

mud banks

fine yellow tiles

tile soffit rafters

Palace Hall, Hue

stone base & floor

Introduction

Introduction

Ancher Mortlock & Woolley

By Jennifer Taylor

For more than 50 years the firm of Ancher Mortlock & Woolley[1] has provided leadership and served as an exemplar for architectural practice in Australia. Its members have not only been involved in practice but have also been committed to teaching, to affairs of the profession, and to fighting for the advancement of design. All in all, Australian architecture is greatly indebted to the consistent commitment of Sydney Ancher and his partners in the period since the firm was founded in 1945.

The firm's architecture is one that combines integrity and creativity; the voice of the firm, from Sydney Ancher to Ken Woolley, has insisted on the art of architecture as its distinguishing characteristic. Ken Woolley spelt this out clearly in his Walter Burley Griffin address of 1997, "Give Art a Chance: Architecture or Mere Building". Always looking forward and welcoming fresh challenges, Ancher Mortlock & Woolley point the way to innovative solutions for the next century in their latest work.

Sydney Ancher, the firm's founder, unquestionably remains one of the most respected and admired architects of recent Australian history. From his pioneering work of the 1930s, when he played a major role in introducing Modern architecture to Australia, through his mature work of the 1940s and 1950s, to the personal expressions of his Coffs Harbour period of the 1960s, Ancher inspired more than a generation of Australian architects.

With the growing reputation of his practice and the increasing demands this brought, Ancher took two younger men, Bryce Mortlock and Stuart Murray, into partnership in 1952. In many ways the interests of the firm widened with the new input as the strengths of each architect lay in diverse directions. Ancher was always happiest with projects of a modest size, while both Mortlock and Murray were confident with multi-storey buildings. Of the tall buildings, Murray's Deepdene Apartments in Elizabeth Bay (1967) are the most memorable.

Mortlock was concerned with large-scale planning and thus introduced quite a different dimension to the office. His contribution was highly significant, notably through the 1965–66 Master Plan for the Engineering Precinct for the University of

Sydney and the 1970 Report on Planning at Melbourne University, which established guidelines based on principles rather than proposing the solution of a master plan. The diversity in the firm's interests increased with the entry of Ken Woolley to the partnership in 1964, as did the extent of work undertaken, the size of the individual projects, and the number of staff, which rose from eight in 1964 to sixty by the end of 1965.

Woolley came from a very successful career in the New South Wales Government Architect's Office where he had designed highly acclaimed large buildings such as the Fisher Library at the University of Sydney (1962, in collaboration with T.E. O'Mahony) and the New South Wales State Government Offices in Sydney (1964). Woolley had also established a reputation for designing housing for the "project developers" and, through his innovative but sensible designs (in both plan and construction), had made a laudable contribution to raising the quality of the commercially available house in Australia. This work, principally for the firm of Pettit & Sevitt, continued after he joined Ancher and was extended to multiple housing for urban sites. The Penthouses, Rushcutters Bay (1967), demonstrated the possibilities of an imaginative stepped solution which enhanced both its locations and the possibilities of inner city living.

The new partners were also responsible for major shifts in the visual aesthetics of the firm's architecture, adding the use of natural materials with an emphasis on craft, characteristic of the Sydney School, to the "white" language of Ancher's buildings. The influences of Le Corbusier's Jaoul Houses, English Brutalism, and the crafted works of Alvar Aalto are evident in the Sydney School buildings and in other work of the late 1950s and 1960s. This can be seen in Mortlock's Badham House (1959), in the firm's design for the RAIA Headquarters Building in Canberra[2], and in several influential works by Woolley, such as his own Mosman house (1962). Transitional was the Northbourne Avenue Housing, Canberra (1959–63), which can be seen both as a summation of Ancher's career dedicated to the aesthetic and ethic of early Modern architecture, and as an example of the collaboration of the younger Murray. In this project the design concepts of the Weissenhof Housing in Stuttgart are combined with Radburn planning principles in a development of mixed medium-density housing types planned around a hierarchical arrangement of access routes. It remains unique as a development example of a large housing complex based on the model of early Modernism translated to Australian conditions.

In the 1960s the firm was commissioned to design a number of major buildings for universities, including several student unions. While Woolley's University of Newcastle Student Union deployed the brick palette of the Sydney School, the major part of the architecture was cast in the sculptural forms of a somewhat subdued concrete Brutalism. Notable examples that introduced this direction to Australia are Mortlock's buildings for the Engineering Precinct of the 1960s and Woolley's Wentworth Building (1968), both for the University of Sydney. Certainly from the 1960s on, much of the work of the firm is characterised by an interest in materials and in the rational use of structure. This is evident in the brick buildings and concrete structures, and then in the variations in the modular use of steel and glass, as in Woolley's Glasshouses for the Royal Botanic Gardens, Sydney (1988), which gently curve across their site.

The partnership was primarily one of independent designers, but a rich personal association developed between Mortlock and Woolley, with each contributing to the mental stimulus and growth of the other. Woolley, in particular, was interested in the intellectual aspects of architecture, in contrast to Ancher who had never cared to theorise about his work. Ancher left the firm in 1965, and by the 1970s Mortlock was increasingly involved with political matters relating to the profession, and Murray was less involved than before, finally leaving in 1976. Consequently Ken Woolley, who had maintained a strong presence in the partnership, assumed more of the responsibility for design. From the end of that decade he became the principal most fully engaged in design for the firm, and it is his work which, from that time on, primarily determined its direction and status. In addition, Woolley had gained a reputation for his broad views and balanced opinions and became sought-after for numerous advisory and adjudicating committees.

The 1970s were also a time of change for Woolley, partly stemming from his further travels in Europe and Asia, with a deepening sense of history and a return to the exploratory sketching which had been both tool and pleasure for him in the 1950s. Woolley had always been interested in transforming the vernacular, and a major input to his thinking came through a four-year involvement with Ron Sevitt on remote indigenous housing and planning research for the RAIA. This took him all over northern and central Australia and developed in him an awareness of the fundamental principles of "what architecture is". He learnt that "housing is what you do after you solve the problems".[3]

While there are constant themes in Woolley's architecture, rarely are there evident visual affiliations across the spectrum of work; the buildings are always particular to site and program. Perhaps it is the houses he designed for himself that best show Woolley's versatility. The 1962 house, with its dark textured materials and raked roof, hid among the timbers of the sloping site. In contrast, the 1981 inner city house at Paddington stood proudly as a white prismatic tower, while the 1986 house in the beachside suburb of Palm Beach assumed the informal dress of timber and corrugated iron. Woolley followed the Wentworth Building with a prominent inner city building, Town Hall House (1971–74), where precast concrete was combined with in-situ sections to produce a lively and varied profile, breaking down the visual impact of the overall mass. Woolley's Sydney School architecture was sensitively related to the natural landscape in form, texture and tone, and with the design of Town Hall House this concern was carried into the urban setting—in this case, primarily nineteenth century sandstone. This specificity is explicit in the rich and subtle design for the Australian Embassy in Bangkok (1973–78), which skilfully marries the colourful tiled and water-bound buildings of that city with the strong horizontal forms of Modern architecture to create a sensuous contemporary work.

Such a visual response to place remains evident in his later work. Demonstrative is the double-skinned Queenscliff Surf Pavilion (1983), which through form and colour creates a transition between the beach scene and the red brick apartment buildings overlooking it. The Park Hyatt Hotel at Campbells Cove, Sydney

(1986-90), which presents a low and curving facade to the harbour, provides a later example of such a sensitive contextual relationship. Since 1989 Woolley has been involved with the intensely contextual Victorian State Library project, involving refurbishment of the early buildings including the domed reading room, the insertion of reserved, complementary blocks adjacent to the principal buildings of the historic fabric, and the addition of infill structures into the internal courtyards. The latter was a delicate operation for which Woolley chose steel framing with dramatic spaceframe roofs. The State Library project, and in particular the large new blocks on the street frontage, is demonstrative of Woolley's consistent, reserved and well-mannered attitude to the setting of his buildings.

Woolley's insistence on the artistic value of architecture has always directed his designs. Demonstrative of this conviction is the Mormon Chapel at Leura (1980), a delightfully free-formed white concrete building, pleasingly fresh in Woolley's handling of form and the quality of light on it and within it. With its pure sculptural and symbolic functions, the 1986 Australian Hellenic War Memorial in Canberra, prepared with Wally Barda, provided another opportunity to pursue this direction. The Memorial is both dramatic and evocative and provides a powerful addition to the sculptural works lining Anzac Parade. The work's symbolism of the futility of war is captured both in the iconic forms and in the nature of the approach and setting. It was the Sydney Airport Control Tower (1992–94), however, that fully demonstrated Woolley's sculptural abilities. The striking geometry of the tower provides a memorable landmark for Sydney's major point of arrival. Consistent with Woolley's Modernist position, the drama of the tower is derived from the external display of the structure spiralling around the central core. The State Hockey Centre, Homebush Bay (1997–98), designed for the 2000 Olympic Games, continues the development of arresting form generated from the exterior celebration of the possibilities of steel construction, with an innovative back-stayed single mast structure holding a roof consisting of metal leaves hinged to each adjoining panel.

Ken Woolley's mature buildings of the late 1980s and early 1990s exhibit a marked confidence in the handling of large civic buildings. The Commonwealth Law Courts, Parramatta (1984–87), and the ABC Radio and Orchestra Centre in Ultimo (1986–90) are commanding works in which Woolley has manipulated the form to enhance the presence of the buildings. In these buildings and others Woolley calls upon the traditional landmark of the tower to bring additional presence to civic edifices. The Blood Bank and Laboratories, Parramatta (1992–95), immediately across the street from the Law Courts, confronts the same issues of scale and presence. In this case the building provides an arresting presence with its dynamic winged profile.

Woolley's most monumental work to date is the series of exhibition halls (stretching 325 metres in length) for the Royal Agricultural Showgrounds at Homebush Bay (1996–98), which are also a major venue for the 2000 Olympic Games. This large building heroically defines one edge of the point of arrival of the train from Sydney, and forms on its other facades, in a very responsive and responsible manner, major urban edges to principal circulation paths. Further drama is added by the corner tower designed to carry dynamic signage and to mark the entry to the Showgrounds. From his earliest buildings, Woolley has had an empathy with timber construction and returns to its use in the arresting structure and detail of the timber laminate and steel composite roofing throughout the halls. Dominating the spatial volumes of the interior is the Great Hall, a dramatic domed space 42 metres high, which is vested with a powerful iconic value by both its size and its traditional form.

Few firms in the history of Australian architecture can approach the sustained performance of Ancher Mortlock & Woolley over the past 50 years. The work has been innovative, artistic, exploratory and responsible, and each member of the partnership has contributed in differing ways to the firm's general excellence of performance. Ken Woolley's most recent work continues the invention and formal strength of the firm's architecture. The Parramatta Blood Bank, the RAS Exhibition Halls and the State Hockey Centre show the ease and confidence with which Woolley rises to challenges, and responds with new materials and fresh forms appropriate to the program and reflective of his time. It is with this confidence and ability that the firm looks ahead to the next century.

[1] After Ken Woolley joined and before Stuart Murray left, the firm was known as Ancher Mortlock Murray & Woolley.

[2] This project was initiated by an invitation to Ancher, but his design was not deemed appropriate by the authorities. The final design came from an amalgamation of input from the other partners.

[3] Conversation, June 1998.

Jennifer Taylor is an architectural critic and historian noted for her writing on Australian and Japanese architecture. She has taught in architectural schools in many countries and is currently at the Queensland University of Technology, Brisbane.

Her writings include *An Australian Identity: Houses for Sydney 1953–63*; *Architecture: A Performing Art* (with John Andrews); *Appropriate Architecture: Ken Woolley*; *Australian Architecture Since 1960*; *World Architecture 1900–2000: A Critical Mosaic*; *Tall Buildings in Australian Cities*; and *Fumihiko Maki*.

She was awarded the Japan Foundation Fellowship in 1975 and 1994–95 and the RAIA Marion Mahony Griffin Inaugural Award for writing and teaching in 1998.

Travel Drawings by Ken Woolley

These travel drawings were partly recreational and partly a pursuit of my interest in urban life, or townscape. Mostly they are in medium point fibre pen on A4 art paper pads, drawing directly without construction lines. Some are in coloured pencil, which is not as immediate as the pen and is more laborious. I like the fibre pen because it is more like a calligraphy brush than a nib, suiting an early training that tended more to painting than drawing. They are mostly about observation and the interest of their subject matter rather than development of the art of drawing—my art remains architecture.

One of the few open spaces in Fez, Morocco, where alleyways intersect beside the mosque

Place Seffarine Fez
Ken Woolley 94

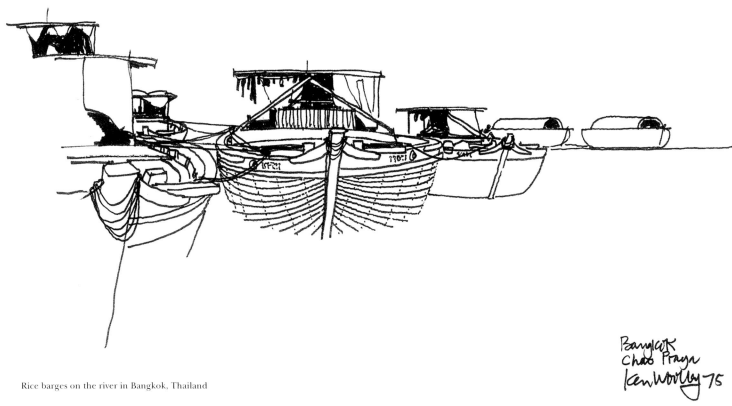

Rice barges on the river in Bangkok, Thailand

Edinburgh Castle, Scotland

Pencil sketch of the abandoned kasbah of Ait Ben Haddou

The ruins of the Theatre of Marcellus in Rome, containing medieval dwellings and a Renaissance palace converted to modern apartments

The lake, city palace and old town of Udaipur in India

The old city of Hanoi, known as the "Thirty-Six Streets", with narrow, very deep "tube" houses

A place with no water in Venice

Campo S. Maria Formosa, Venice
Ken Woolley 85

Bridge on the Isle Saint Louis, Paris

The hilltop town of Taormina, in Sicily

Courtyards in the Mogul fort at Agra, India

Old restaurant in the bazaar above the Bosporus, Turkey

Architectural Drawings by Ken Woolley

These perspective drawings of projects are
mostly from earlier in my career when
I had either more energy or more time.
I once made money as a perspectivist, which
is how I met Brian Pettit and Ron Sevitt.

Perspective of the GMLS Building and the West Amenities Building, Garden Island, Sydney

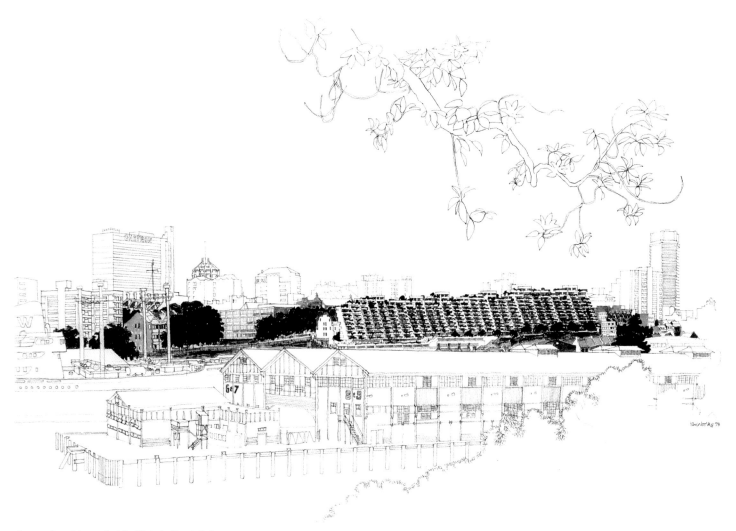

Perspective of the project for Victoria Street, Sydney

Perspective of the Australian Embassy project, Bangkok

Perspective of Town Hall House and Sydney Square

shadow line

pit

Canan at Jaipur
Jantar Mantar

Early Works of Ancher Mortlock & Murray

This selection of buildings represents
some of the high standard, indeed
pioneering, work which helped establish
Modern architecture in Australia, and is
typical of the work of Ancher Mortlock
& Murray prior to my joining the firm.

Sydney Ancher House

Design/Completion 1945/1946
Killara, Sydney, New South Wales
Ancher family
120 square metres
Brick, concrete floors, timber roof
Painted brick, slate roof, painted timber windows

This was Ancher's own house and the foundation of his practice. There could not be a greater contrast between this approach, hugging the ground and growing out of the site context, and that of the 1950s houses by Harry Seidler. One is incorporated in the site, the other perches on it. The two architects are regarded as the main forces in establishing Modern architecture in Sydney, and these two strands persist in Sydney architecture today.

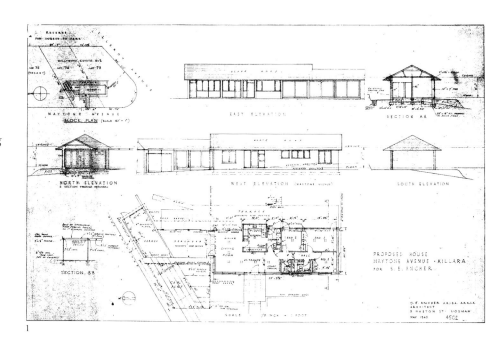

1   Original working drawing
2   Rear of house in bushland setting

1

2

Hamill House

Design/Completion 1947/1949
Killara, Sydney, New South Wales
Hamill family
120 square metres
Brick, concrete floors, timber roof
Painted brick, concrete roof tiles, painted timber windows

Hamill House is one of the most admired examples of Ancher's work, which established Modern architecture in Sydney immediately after the war. It is one of a group of three houses built together, each quite small due to post-war austerity building restrictions.

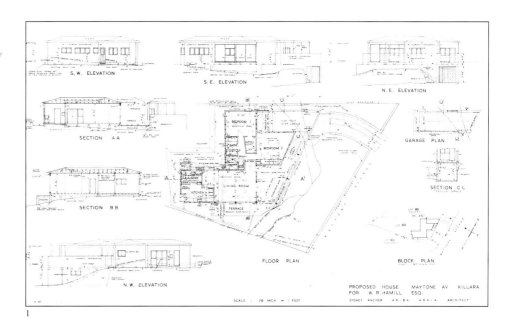

1   Original working drawing
2   Front of house in bushland setting

1

2

Badham House

Design/Completion 1959/1960
Cronulla, New South Wales
Dr Badham
300 square metres
Timber frame and load-bearing brick
Stained timber frame and windows, grey cement bricks, fibre cement panels

Badham House was a significant departure by Bryce Mortlock from the pristine white character of the houses designed by Ancher.

1

2

1   North porch and pool
2   North porch and pool by night
Opposite:
    Internal courtyard

Northbourne Avenue Housing

Design/Completion 1959/1963
Canberra, Australian Capital Territory
National Capital Development Commission
169 apartments and townhouses (average size approx. 100 square metres)
Brick and concrete
Stucco render, painted timber

Northbourne Avenue Housing was Sydney Ancher's only design for group housing and was one of the first public housing groups of any significance in Australia. It is now under threat of demolition.

1

2

3

1 Small tower blocks
2 Maisonette units
3 Townhouses
4 Pergolas and connecting pathways

4

Civil Engineering Building

Design/Completion 1961/1963
Sydney, New South Wales
University of Sydney, Darlington Precinct
Reinforced concrete and steel
Face brick, off-form concrete, steel

This was the first completed building in Bryce Mortlock's master plan for the new Engineering Precinct at the University of Sydney, which involved the expansion of the campus across City Road into Darlington. The building was important in helping the practice move beyond domestic-scale work, and led to rapid expansion, with Ken Woolley joining the firm in 1964.

1

1   General view
2   Civil Engineering Building courtyard

2

Elizabeth Bay Apartments

Design/Completion 1967/1971
Elizabeth Bay, New South Wales
Whaling Road Investments Pty Ltd
Two double-storey apartments (280 square metres); single-level penthouse
(110 square metres)
Precast concrete, load-bearing wall panels and prestressed concrete, T-beam
floor panels
Exposed aggregate precast concrete, aluminium window frames

The Elizabeth Bay Apartments are a distinctive building by Stuart Murray, reflecting his particular interest in urbanism and planning.

The highly individual building form expresses the many influences of its program: client requirements for separate entrances, privacy and security; and the existing street environment of exclusive apartments and large private houses. Its form is moulded by the shape of the site and by the implications of the city council restrictions regarding setbacks, coverage and height. The north face of the building is all glass, with balconies facing north to a panoramic view of Sydney Harbour.

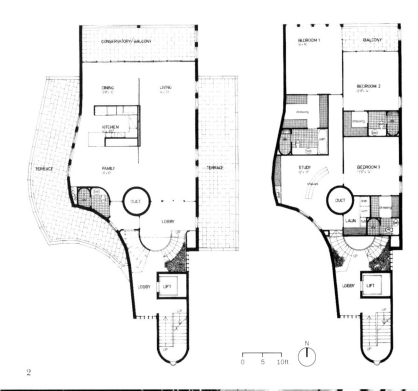

2

1 Balconies facing Sydney Harbour
2 Lower and upper level floor plans
3 Entrance from Elizabeth Bay Road

1

3

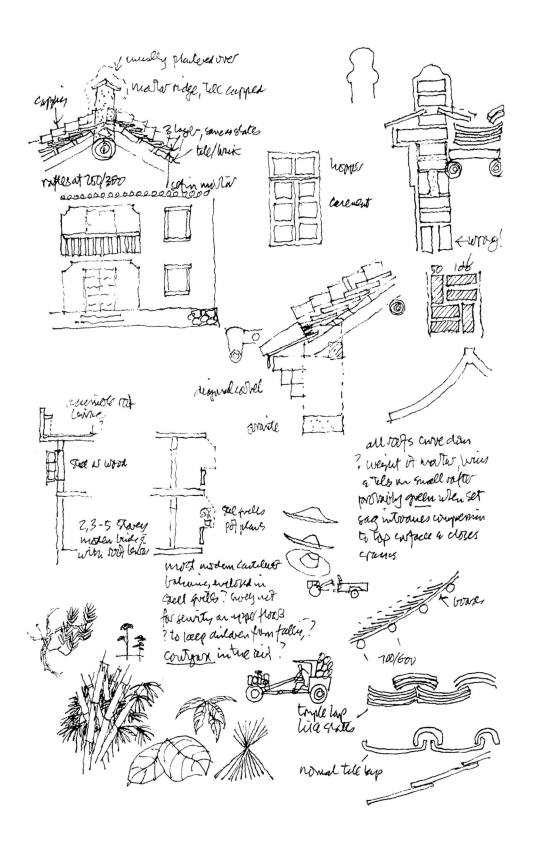

Early Works of Ken Woolley, Architect

This group of projects shows some of my early work in the Government Architect's Office and my first house, at Mosman.

Chapel and Sisters' Home, St Margaret's Hospital

Design/Completion 1955/1958
Darlinghurst, Sydney, New South Wales
St Margaret's Maternity Hospital
500 square metres
Precast concrete, reinforced concrete, load-bearing brickwork
Timber, steel, copper roof, steel windows, glass blocks, face brick

This was the first building Ken Woolley designed independently and the first to be built. The circular chapel is on the upper floor, over a garden lounge room. It is linked by a narthex to the Sisters' Home, which is simply six floors of bedrooms built with cross-wall, load-bearing brickwork.

The chapel is 16 metres in diameter and consists of precast panels, like barrel staves but staggered, with a narrow window of glass blocks between each. At the top the panels are tied by a ring beam which carries radiating steel trusses with a compression ring of timber struts and a suspended tension ring at the middle. A roof lantern and a cross are positioned immediately above. The timber purlins are laid like a spider web, increasing in depth with the radiating span. A copper roof completes the volume. This approach to lighting around the edges of the formal elements has persisted through most of Ken Woolley's subsequent work.

The chapel's circular form served three roles, providing a foil to the rectangular residential section, a contemplative interior space, and a distinctive focus at the converging point of the adjoining hospital buildings.

1

1   Interior view
2   Street view

2

Fisher Library, University of Sydney, Camperdown

Design/Completion 1958/1962
Sydney, New South Wales
University of Sydney
Joint architects: NSW Government Architect & T.E. O'Mahony;
Government Design Architect: Ken Woolley
27,000 square metres
Flat-plate lift-slab concrete floor, steel columns
Bronze extruded window frames and column cladding, sandstone panels,
rubber floors, Tasmanian blackwood panelling

The Fisher Library was originally designed when Cobden Parkes was Government Architect, and was completed under Ted Farmer. Dr Andrew Osborn, the new librarian from Harvard, wanted a completely new approach for Australian university libraries. The plan has an entry link between two contrasting buildings: one with a large open floor plan, continuous windows and reading areas around the perimeter; the other with a dense, limited-access bookstack with slit windows at each aisle between the books.

The use of bronze for windows and cladding was later applied extensively in the State Office Block. It was found that by keeping bronze members small and simple, utilising their greater strength, the cost was comparable to larger, more complex aluminium sections. The library was the first fully air-conditioned building at the university.

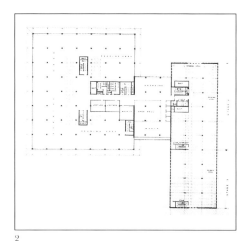

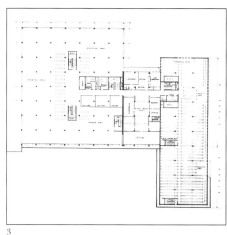

2

3

1 Entrance hall and atrium
2 Level 2 plan
3 Level 4 plan
4 North facade with cantilevered floors

1

4

Woolley House, Mosman

Design/Completion 1961/1962
Mosman, Sydney, New South Wales
Ken Woolley
180 square metres
Brick walls, concrete floors, timber roof beams
Terracotta tile roof, cork tile and coir mat floors, plaster and vinyl bathroom,
timber windows

This project combined for the first time a number of themes Ken Woolley had developed in previous work: the regular, modulating grid; the metaphorical central idea ("like garden terraces stepping down the hillside"); the sidestepping walls providing visual layers while accommodating diagonal movement; and the appearance of irregularity through variation within a controlled order. Other significant features include the controlled perception of the natural site; the direct and iconoclastic detailing; the accommodation of necessarily inconsistent items, like kitchen equipment; and the white plaster bathroom shell. The latter reappears as a technique in the University of Newcastle Union kitchen and service, and eventually as the whole interior of the Seventh Day Adventist Church (1971).

The materials have a tactile quality, particularly the brickwork, which is like a gently textured rug and not at all aggressive or crude. For the first time there emerges an interest in contextual and historical references, notably to the bungalow style.

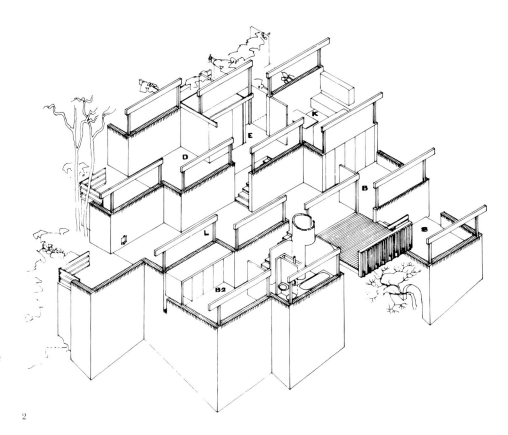

2

1

3

1   View from adjoining gardens
2   Isometric
3   South and west elevations
4   Cross-section
5   Interior

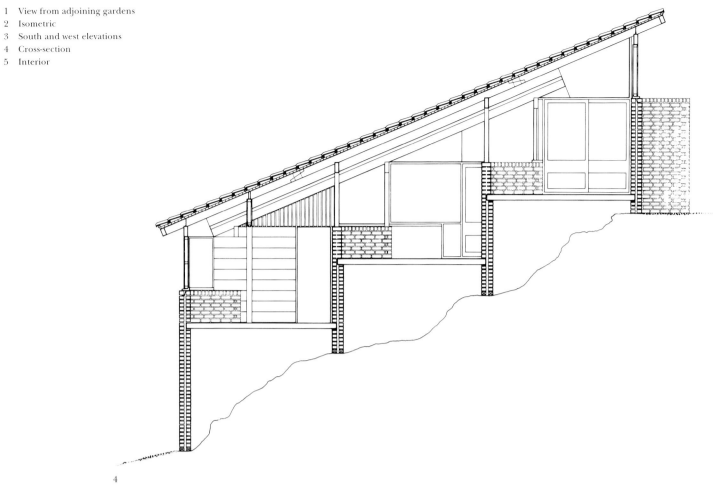

4

5

State Office Block

Design/Completion 1960/1965
Sydney, New South Wales
NSW Government Architect: E.H. Farmer
Government Design Architect: Ken Woolley
50,000 square metres
Steel and concrete composite, lift-form concrete core and steel floor beams, cellular steel floor, and steel and concrete columns
Cladding of pre-weathered roll-formed bronze sheet; extruded bronze window frames with zip gaskets and heat-absorbing glass; black granite and brown/grey reconstructed granite precast panels
Interiors of white mosaic tile, black bean timber panelling and carpet

The tower of the State Office Block evolved from an interest in pure geometric shape, being exactly square in plan. A central core carried the wind loads, expressed by the elliptical arched webs across the lobbies. The lower wings related to the height of the adjoining buildings and the whole character of Macquarie Street, reflecting a desire to link the building into the existing city fabric. The colour also responded to the brown sandstone, copper-roofed character of the older part of the city, particularly the government buildings. The external columns and projecting floors provided sun control and cleaning access and improved wind qualities.

The State Office Block sought to be an important statement in government building, comparable with the nearby Chief Secretary's Building, Lands Department, Treasury and State Library. The strict modular planning extended from the four-inch grid on which the grooves in the bronze panelling were set out, through to the usual ceiling, room and column grids, reflecting an early concern to maintain the integrity of a flexible office mechanism. This was a much more durable building than was normal for the city. It had a floorspace ratio of about 8:1, although it was 10:1 by the method used at the time. The building and its spiral fountain were recently demolished to make way for a commercial and residential development.

1

2

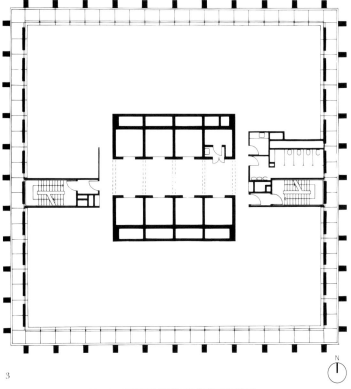

3

1 Facade showing external columns and overhangs
2 Tower from the Botanic Gardens, with Macquarie Street in the foreground
3 Typical floor plan
4 Spiral fountain
5 Lift core
6 Vestibule
7 Theatre interior

4

5

6

7

boat harbour

rocky inlet point

Concepts for the golf course at Shensen, China

Works of
Ancher Mortlock & Woolley

The notebook drawings within this section
concurrently explore concept and detail
in all the active projects. They are small
fibre pen drawings, usually done away
from the office, and are almost a stream
of consciousness in architectural terms.
They are used to seek and work out
concepts and the development of ideas
and then convey them to my colleagues.

It is usual for the detail of one project to
appear on the same page as concept ideas
for others. The tiny scale of the drawings
eliminates the irrelevant and reflects the
fact that they are a thought process, not a
means of presentation. Not all the projects
are illustrated with their concept sketches,
as quite often the concept evolved in
a different medium.

Pettit & Sevitt Houses

Production period 1962–1978
Mostly Sydney, New South Wales; also other states
Pettit & Sevitt (project builders)
3,500 houses built (average size about 150 square metres)
Timber frame, brick veneer
Brick, stained timber boarding, concrete tile or steel deck roofs

After small beginnings in competition and exhibition houses, Brian Pettit and Ron Sevitt took up the opportunity to develop a modern house vernacular. Clients could select a house from a demonstration group and have it architect-adapted to their own site and needs. They were remarkably receptive to the standards of materials finish and colour, and even to the furnishing and landscape, which became exhibition attractions in their own right.

More than 1,500 examples were built of one design—the lowline, flat-roofed and most "modern" of all the houses. Eventually Pettit and Sevitt were invited into government housing and we were able to experiment with small lot and courtyard groups. When the supply of inner urban land ran out in the larger cities, the market declined and the trend to renovating older housing gathered pace.

1 Demonstration village
2 Lowline House floor plan
3 Lowline House
4 Lowline House interior

1

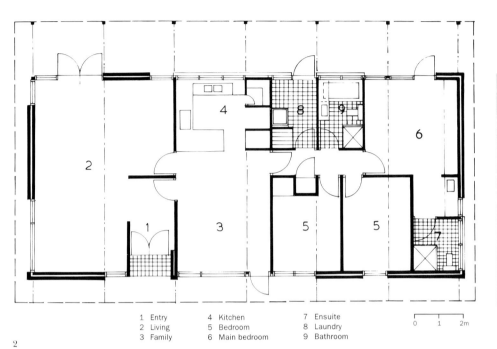

1 Entry   4 Kitchen   7 Ensuite
2 Living   5 Bedroom   8 Laundry
3 Family   6 Main bedroom   9 Bathroom

0   1   2m

2

3

4

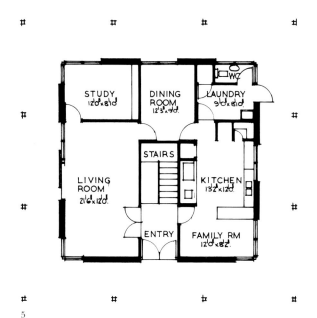

STUDY
12'0"x8'0"

DINING ROOM
12'3"x9'0"

LAUNDRY
9'0"x8'0"

WC

STAIRS

LIVING ROOM
21'6"x12'0"

KITCHEN
13'2"x12'0"

ENTRY

FAMILY RM
12'0"x8'2"

5

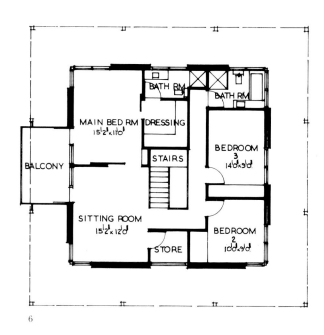

BATH RM

BATH RM

MAIN BED RM
15'2"x11'0"

DRESSING

BEDROOM 3
14'0"x9'0"

BALCONY

STAIRS

SITTING ROOM
15'2"x12'0"

STORE

BEDROOM 2
10'0"x9'0"

6

7

8

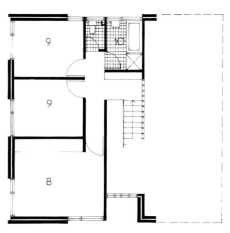

1 Entry   6 Study
2 Living   7 Laundry
3 Dining   8 Main bedroom
4 Family   9 Bedroom
5 Kitchen   10 Bathroom

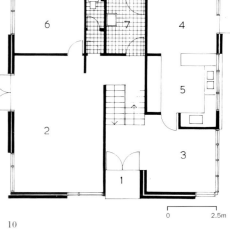

0   2.5m

10

9

5   Large House ground floor plan
6   Large House first floor plan
7   Large House
8   Split-level House with SL2 and others behind
9   Big Split-level House
10   Big Split-level House floor plans

F.C. Pye Field Environment Laboratory

Design/Completion 1965/1966
Black Mountain, Canberra, Australian Capital Territory
Commonwealth Scientific and Industrial Research Organisation (CSIRO)
1,670 square metres
Reinforced concrete, steel roof
Off-form concrete, face blockwork, timber linings and ceilings

1   Entrance facade
2   Glass-roofed courtyard
3   Levels 1–3 floor plans
4   Entrance detail
5   Colloquium room
Opposite:
    Service area and exit stair

It was a requirement that the building should possess a certain architectural elegance reflecting the generosity of the benefactor after whom it is named, as well as satisfying an unusual set of technical requirements calling for three distinct orders of use: rough workshops, laboratories and research offices.

The workshops (including wind tunnel and mobile laboratories) occupy the basement, utilising the fall of the land for level access. The laboratories on the ground floor are controlled environments, protected from outside influence, blank-walled to the exterior, and introspective. The offices on the top level look out through continuous strip windows under wide, overhanging eaves.

The compact square plan encloses a glass-roofed inner court which acts as a focus for the laboratories and a place for experimental planting. The main entrance opens directly into this court at laboratory level. Adjustable sun control louvres to the roof allow solar contribution to winter heating.

All finishes are simple and direct, being in most cases the structural elements themselves. Elaborate detail and paintwork have been avoided.

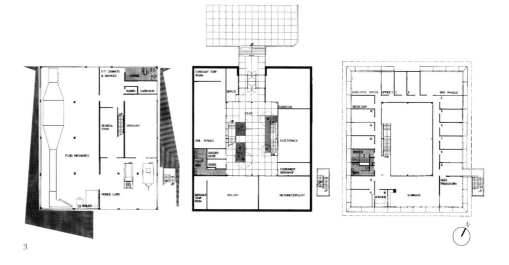

3

4

1

2

5

The Penthouses

Design/Completion 1965/1968
Darling Point, Sydney, New South Wales
Sebel family
2,000 square metres (12 units of 150–180 square metres each)
Load-bearing brick and concrete
Painted walls, terracotta tiled roofs and terraces

The project illustrates the important aspects of medium-density housing. For people to forgo their normal house, a townhouse has to be superior in locality, offering better transport and access to amenities. It also has to provide an acceptable area of private outdoor space, with sun and any available views.

In detached houses, usually only a small part of the garden is visually and acoustically private; this function can easily be reproduced in higher density housing. The remainder of a normal garden is usually a form of display or an address point—a means of personal expression and individuality which also serves a civic streetscape role. In a townhouse group, these functions can be achieved by the development as a whole.

In the Penthouses development, individuality and variety find expression in the means of access to each dwelling. Entrances are differentiated in location and treatment. Access paths traverse and climb the hillside and small courts and terraces lead to the doorways, while each outside space is on the roof of the dwellings below. This overlapping terraced design became a common solution in Sydney, where steep sites with water views are numerous.

2

1 Access steps between the buildings
2 View from Yarranabee Park
3 Section
4 Site plan
5 Private terrace shielded by overhangs

1

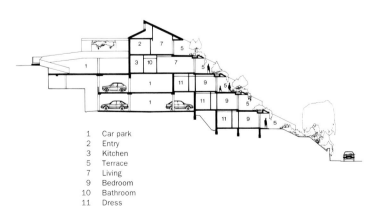

1   Car park
2   Entry
3   Kitchen
5   Terrace
7   Living
9   Bedroom
10 Bathroom
11 Dress

3

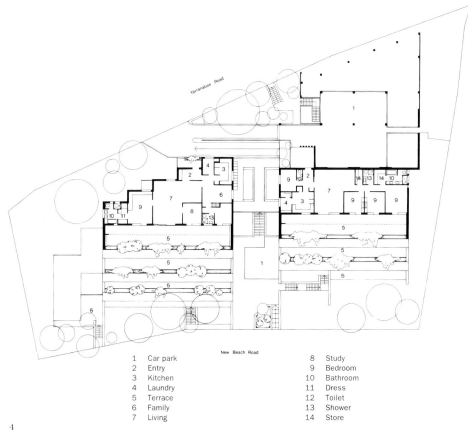

1	Car park	8	Study
2	Entry	9	Bedroom
3	Kitchen	10	Bathroom
4	Laundry	11	Dress
5	Terrace	12	Toilet
6	Family	13	Shower
7	Living	14	Store

4

5

The Cottages

Design/Completion 1966/1968
Cremorne Point, Sydney, New South Wales
Strata Development Corporation
Six houses (850 square metres)
Brick veneer with timber frame and floors
Concrete, painted brick, timber, plasterboard, concrete roof tiles

This project replaced one old cottage with six. In the early days of townhouse development in Sydney, it tested various assumptions about privacy and screening and set a benchmark for later projects. A pathway links the street with common areas and the car park, and serves the individual entrance porches to each house. To maximise the available space, each house was designed in an L shape to enclose a private court. The building design and expression were drawn directly from experiences in concurrent detached housing, notably for Pettit and Sevitt, with the scale and nature of the group being related to the character of Cremorne Point. Sandstone walls from the foundations of the previous building were recycled.

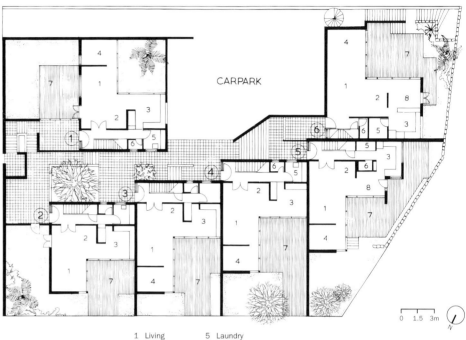

1 Living	5 Laundry
2 Dining	6 Toilet
3 Kitchen	7 Courtyard
4 Study	8 Family

1

2

1 Site and floor plan
2 Cluster view from Milson Road
3 Access pathway to each house
4 Private courtyard
5 Courtyards along the boundary

3

4

5

Seventh Day Adventist Church

Design/Completion 1967/1971
Turner, Australian Capital Territory
National Seventh Day Adventist Church
441 square metres
Load-bearing brick, steel roof
Brick paving and compacted river gravel; carpet on timber boarding; red Bowral bricks (external); white painted rendered brick (internal); roll-formed brown-coloured steel decking; built-up flat roofs; white painted plasterboard; stained western red cedar
RAIA Twenty-Five Year Award 1996

The client required a new church auditorium plus meeting and service rooms. The existing building was to be retained as a church hall. The solution involved adopting the comparatively mundane red-brown brick of the existing hall and forming an inward-looking group of buildings with space for people to gather both indoors and outdoors.

Part of the solution came from the nature of the church itself, whose liturgy emphasises baptism, preaching, singing and discussion. The familiar cross symbolism was avoided; instead, it is sufficient that the building is clearly a place for people to gather. The 45-degree roof pitch of the existing hall was adopted for the church and forms a simple triangular prism of brick, rising from a forecourt formed by the old hall and a link composed of meeting and service rooms.

The colour and form of the exterior are designed to avoid competing with or overpowering the nearby Lutheran church. Internally, everything but the floor is white. The form and light are related to the function of baptism, with the whole roof rising on massive buttresses from a pool in the forecourt. The simple landscape treatment accepts the existing scene of wide lawns and rows of deciduous trees. A small brick-paved gathering place is added, with a pool and a few plane trees.

2

1

3

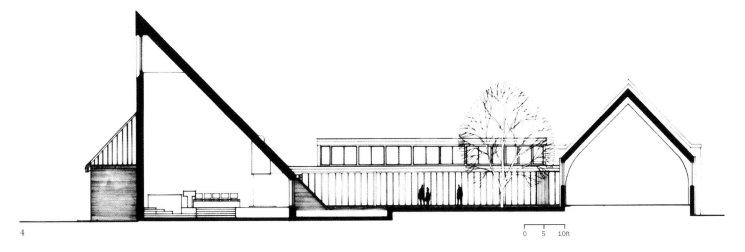

4

1 Choir gallery and concealed window
2 Distant view of the two churches
3 Street view and juxtaposition with the Lutheran church
4 Section
5 Courtyard and entry to the narthex, with classroom gallery behind
6 Courtyard and symbolic pool; note the people in the church sitting lower than the water level

5

6

7 Floor plan
8 Emerging from the dressing area to the immersion font
9 Classroom gallery leading to the church
Opposite:
  Reflected light in the church

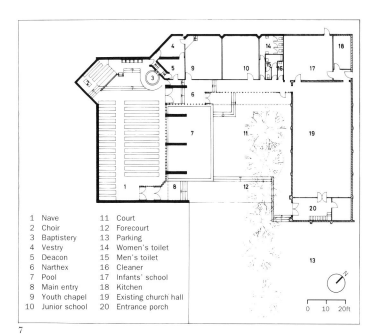

1	Nave	11	Court
2	Choir	12	Forecourt
3	Baptistery	13	Parking
4	Vestry	14	Women's toilet
5	Deacon	15	Men's toilet
6	Narthex	16	Cleaner
7	Pool	17	Infants' school
8	Main entry	18	Kitchen
9	Youth chapel	19	Existing church hall
10	Junior school	20	Entrance porch

7

8

9

University of Newcastle Student Union

Design/Completion 1964/1970 (three stages)
Shortland Campus, Newcastle, New South Wales
University of Newcastle
2,262 square metres (Stage 1)
Load-bearing brickwork, timber trusses
Brick, precast concrete, timber, terracotta roof tiles

The University of Newcastle Student Union was Ken Woolley's first commission on entering private practice, resulting from interest generated by the Fisher Library and the Mosman House. It sought to take some of the themes of the house and look at the possibilities of using them in a much larger building.

The design idea was to start at one finished edge and work away from it as needed at different stages in a rambling, informal and adaptable way, using courtyards and galleries as a circulation structure. The servicing and kitchens form an expandable pivot around which the extension could occur.

1

2

3

1 Original entrance side
2 Kitchen with rooflights and vents
3 Student Union building after completion of the three main stages
4 Brickwork detail
5 Access gallery around the courtyards

4

5

University of Newcastle Staff Club

Design/Completion 1967/1968
Newcastle, New South Wales
University of Newcastle
454 square metres
Load-bearing brick walls, steel and timber roof construction
Brick, concrete, timber, glazed terracotta

The Staff House was required to provide
dining and recreational facilities for
university staff. The building forms part
of a group with the Student Union and
with it completes one side of the main
central space of the university plan.
A strong relationship exists between the
form, materials and siting of the two
buildings. The Student Union is large and
irregular in outline; to maintain the scale,
the Staff House form is extremely simple
with bold fenestration. The shell-like
containment of highly finished surfaces in
functional areas such as kitchens, serveries
and toilets follows the pattern of the
Woolley House, and the Myers House
in Mosman.

1   Staff Club from the car park
2   Level 2 floor plan of Staff Club and Union
    Building
Opposite:
    Staff Club

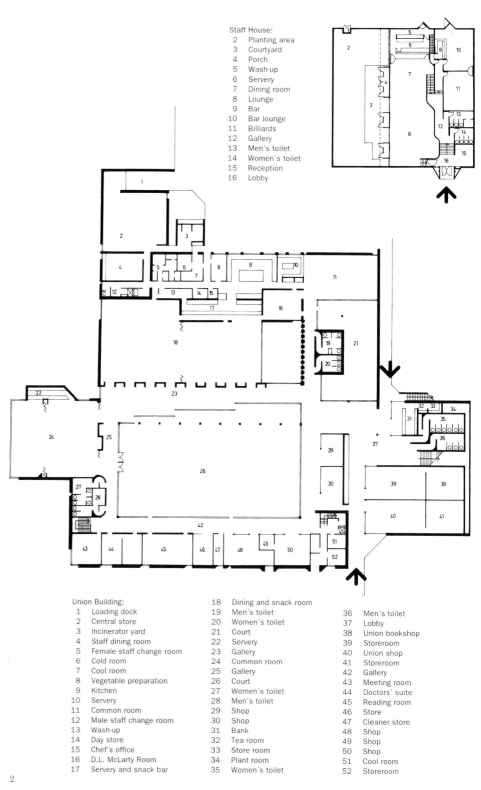

Staff House:
2   Planting area
3   Courtyard
4   Porch
5   Wash-up
6   Servery
7   Dining room
8   Lounge
9   Bar
10 Bar lounge
11 Billiards
12 Gallery
13 Men's toilet
14 Women's toilet
15 Reception
16 Lobby

Union Building:
1   Loading dock
2   Central store
3   Incinerator yard
4   Staff dining room
5   Female staff change room
6   Cold room
7   Cool room
8   Vegetable preparation
9   Kitchen
10 Servery
11 Common room
12 Male staff change room
13 Wash-up
14 Day store
15 Chef's office
16 D.L. McLarty Room
17 Servery and snack bar
18 Dining and snack room
19 Men's toilet
20 Women's toilet
21 Court
22 Servery
23 Gallery
24 Common room
25 Gallery
26 Court
27 Women's toilet
28 Men's toilet
29 Shop
30 Shop
31 Bank
32 Tea room
33 Store room
34 Plant room
35 Women's toilet
36 Men's toilet
37 Lobby
38 Union bookshop
39 Storeroom
40 Union shop
41 Storeroom
42 Gallery
43 Meeting room
44 Doctors' suite
45 Reading room
46 Store
47 Cleaner store
48 Shop
49 Shop
50 Shop
51 Cool room
52 Storeroom

Town Hall House, Sydney Square and Town Hall Refurbishment

Design/Completion 1971/1974
Sydney, New South Wales
Sydney City Council
36,000 square metres
Precast concrete and concrete
Etched, load-bearing, precast concrete facades, aluminium-framed windows, bluestone base

Town Hall House is located on a corner of the Sydney Square civic precinct, which contains the existing Town Hall and St Andrew's Cathedral among other buildings. The design brief required an office building for Sydney City Council staff, public contacts and Town Hall patrons. The acoustics and air-conditioning of the concert hall were upgraded, the Victorian interiors of the existing Town Hall building were restored, and a forecourt was constructed with entrances to the underground railway station.

In cooperation with the consultants for the adjacent St Andrew's House, the entire complex of Sydney Square was developed as a series of connections with the principal roads, and as a network of underground pedestrian arcades connected to the railway system. By removing a clutter of additions, a clear setting was created for the heritage buildings of the Town Hall and St Andrew's Cathedral as well as a much-needed place for public assembly.

The removal of overcrowded offices in the old Town Hall allowed the restoration of the major rooms to their original style and provided space that could be utilised with the adjacent concert hall for service, restaurant and terrace areas.

1

2

1   Drawing of Town Hall House and Sydney Square
    (by Ken Woolley)
2   Town Hall House and Sydney Square with
    St Andrew's Cathedral on the left
3   Town Hall complex and Sydney Square
4   Steps to lower square
5   Details of facade remodelling

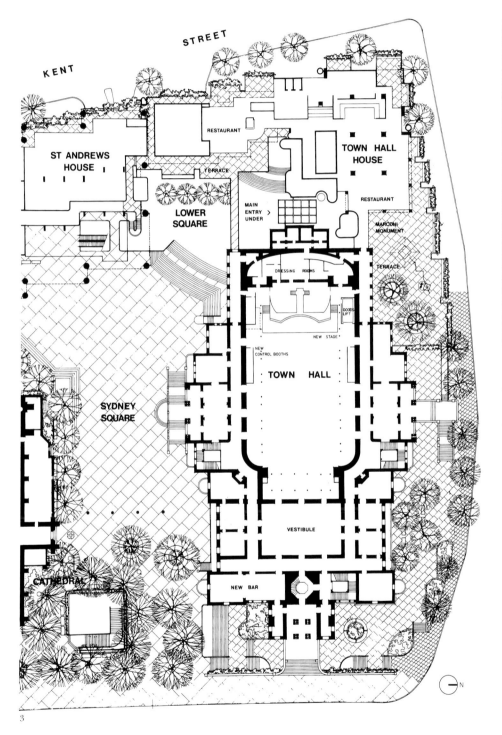

KENT STREET

ST ANDREWS HOUSE

RESTAURANT

TERRACE

LOWER SQUARE

MAIN ENTRY UNDER

TOWN HALL HOUSE

RESTAURANT

MARCONI MONUMENT

TERRACE

DRESSING ROOMS

GOODS LIFT

NEW STAGE

NEW CONTROL BOOTHS

TOWN HALL

SYDNEY SQUARE

VESTIBULE

NEW BAR

CATHEDRAL

3

4

5

Phillip Health Centre and Library, Woden Town Centre

Design/Completion 1972/1975
Woden Town Centre, Canberra, Australian Capital Territory
National Capital Development Commission
4,033 square metres (health centre); 3,286 square metres (library)
Reinforced concrete with steel roofs
Light stone-coloured concrete block and precast concrete

The Phillip Health Centre is a series of professional suites and public health agencies arranged around a two-storey atrium space used for orientation and access. The plan is of the pinwheel corridor type. The library also has a two-storey top-lit space as a foyer adjoining the public way and contains public and children's libraries, a cafe and a community hall.

As a result of a wind study carried out to examine problems caused by a tower block in the Woden Town Centre, a deep pergola was included to improve conditions in the pedestrian spaces around the new library and health centre. With the design based on the visual strength of the precast concrete pergola, the walls are very simple and economical, with variations played on various kinds of openings in light stone-coloured concrete block and precast concrete facades.

1   Library foyer

1

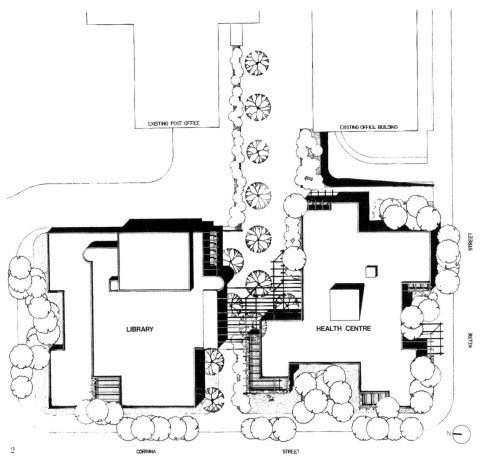

2   Site plan
3   Pathway between library (right) and health centre
    (left)
4   Health centre, level 1 plan
5   Library, level 1 plan
6   View across the small square, from the library to
    the health centre

EXISTING POST OFFICE

EXISTING OFFICE BUILDING

LIBRARY

HEALTH CENTRE

KELTIE STREET

CORINNA STREET

N

2

3

4

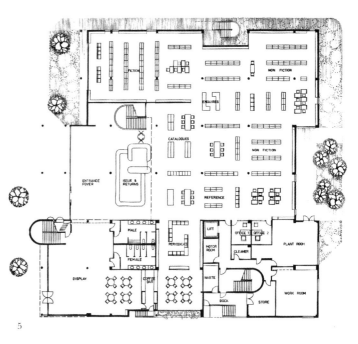

5

6

Wentworth Student Union Building, Sydney University

Design/Completion 1968/1972
Sydney, New South Wales
Sydney University Union and Sydney University Women's Union
5,870 square metres: 1,532 square metres (Stage 1); 2,144 square metres (Stage 2); 2,194 square metres (Stage 3)
Reinforced concrete
Off-form, sandblasted concrete, white ceramic tile, steel windows and screens

In contrast with the Newcastle and Macquarie Student Unions, this was a completely urban site, separated from the main university by an expressway. An existing pedestrian bridge spanning the expressway had to be picked up in the first stage of the new Student Union in order to make it a portal to the developing university precinct in Darlington. The first stage front and rear facades responded to the large-scale dynamics of the freeway and bridges, and set up an architectural vocabulary from which the final stage could be developed.

The pedestrian concourse runs right through the building, changing levels to join another bridge at the rear. It gives access to the Union facilities on the way, intersecting with another internal street leading from the side road entrances.

The materials—concrete with white elements (for which tile was chosen)— were specified by the university for the focal buildings in the new precinct, which was otherwise to be brick and concrete. The large draped roof light of the central space is covered with copper, echoing the architect's use of that material in St Margaret's Chapel, Queenscliff Surf Club and the Parramatta Courts.

2

1

3

1 Interior, Stage 2 dining area
2 City Road elevation
3 Stage 2 from the courtyard
4 Level 1 floor plan
5 Level 2 floor plan
6 Level 5 floor plan

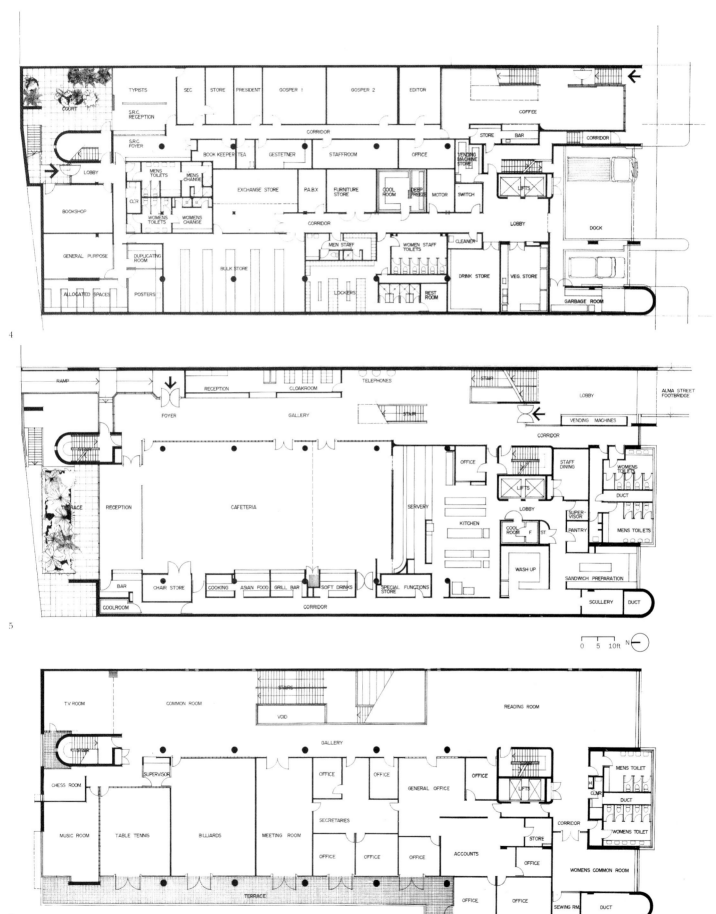

7   Atrium and circulation space (1972)
Opposite:
   City Road facade detail

7

Macquarie Fields Attached Housing

Design/Completion 1973/1974
Macquarie Fields, New South Wales
Housing Commission of New South Wales
108 houses (average size 140 square metres)
Residential blockwork and timber frame, concrete tile and metal roofs
White-painted brick, brown brick, grey block, white and brown tile roofs, fibre cement fascias to flat roofs and for wall planking, fibreglass bolt-on hoods over entrances, aluminium window frames

The Macquarie Fields houses are part of a large Housing Commission estate. A population density of 50 persons per acre (124 persons per hectare) was required to provide an alternative lifestyle located in proximity to new schools, shops and playing fields.

The houses are generally paired so that access between front and rear courtyards could be provided. Due to the higher density of the development and the economic group of the occupants, it was anticipated that courtyards would be used for family activities, growing vegetables, and possibly carrying out trades. Caravans, trailers and sheds had to be accommodated.

There are three basic house designs. The two-storey house has three bedrooms and a bathroom upstairs, and living room, kitchen and laundry downstairs. Access to private courtyards is from the living room, and access to service courts is from the laundry. Entrance doors are generally reached from semi-private alcoves off small common courtyards. All common space is directly overlooked from windows and entrance doors.

The second design is a single-storey L-shaped atrium house with an inward pitched roof, in two- and three-bedroom versions. Accommodation and courts are similar to the other houses. A third, split-level design used on the steeper sloping sections of the site is similar to the single-storey house.

1   Housing seen across parkland
2   Site plan
3   Detail of two-storey row houses
4   One cluster from pedestrian route

1

Australian Embassy, Bangkok

Design/Completion 1973/1978
Bangkok, Thailand
Department of Administrative Services, Overseas Property Bureau
17,000 square metres
Reinforced concrete with diagrid beam floors supported from circular concrete columns on deep precast concrete piles
Facades clad in yellow glazed ceramic tile, local stone bases and landscape walls, local slate paving, steel and aluminium shade roofs

There are two common approaches to the design of embassy buildings. One is to recreate the architecture of the home country in order to identify the building as a symbol; the other is to design a typical International Modern style building. In the Australian case, even if it were appropriate, no combination of traditional architecture and modern functional requirements could relate to the tropical climate of Thailand. Instead, the special qualities of the site and the general environmental qualities of the city suggested a solution generated by the local context.

New buildings in Bangkok are usually built on filled ground, and are raised to prevent flooding. In the design of the Australian Embassy, the local use of water landscape is adopted by virtually flooding the site and standing the buildings in water. As well as providing the building with a beautiful setting, this has the advantage of overcoming problems of flooding before they occur. The site is transformed into a large pond or lake with a series of islands, adding to its security and serving to physically separate the activities of the official residence from those of the chancery. The water landscape generates cool air flow upwards through the main courtyard of the chancery.

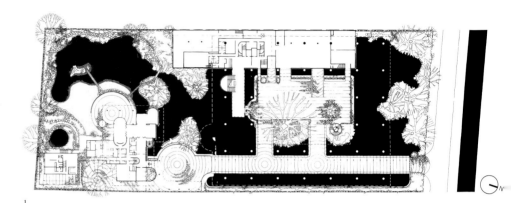
1

2

1   Site plan
2   Ambassador's residence and water garden
3   Existing rainforest trees were incorporated in the water garden between the street and the chancery
4   Private quarters, terrace of the residence

3

4

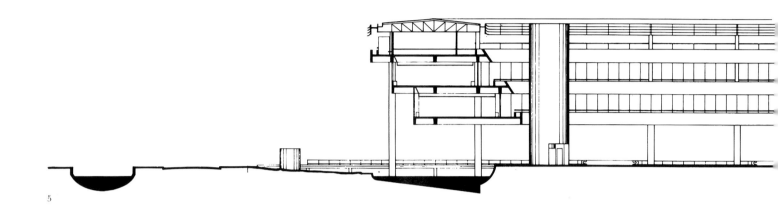

5

6

7

8

5 Section
6 Formal dining room of the residence
7 Moat between the chancery and the street
8 Entrance causeway
9 Rear garden of the residence

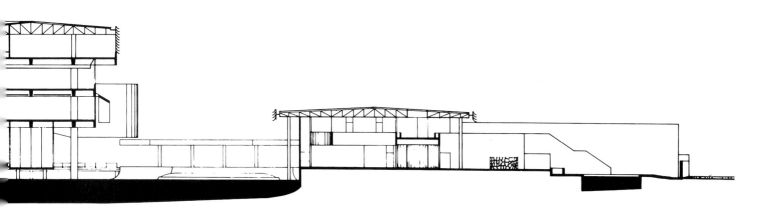

Vila Radio Station, Vanuatu

Design/Completion 1977/1981
Vila, Vanuatu
Australian Government
948 square metres
Reinforced concrete, steel roof
Coloured plaster, aluminium windows, steel roofing

The Australian Aid Program donated radio stations and communications equipment to the two independent nations of Vanuatu and the Solomon Islands. A consortium was formed with communications, broadcasting and engineering experts and Ove Arup and Partners to carry out both projects.

The site for the Vanuatu Radio Station is adjacent to the existing studio facilities on a cliff top with views over Port Vila Harbour. There is a significant fall across the site, which led to the adoption of a part two-storey building. The building is planned so that the central equipment room forms a nucleus for the technical area and provides an acoustic and environmental buffer between the studio/ control rooms and the garage and mechanical plant areas.

1 Downhill side of cliff-top site
2 Floor plans
3 Entrance with large public studio
4 Courtyard of the studio area
5 Detail of lower storey
6 Section

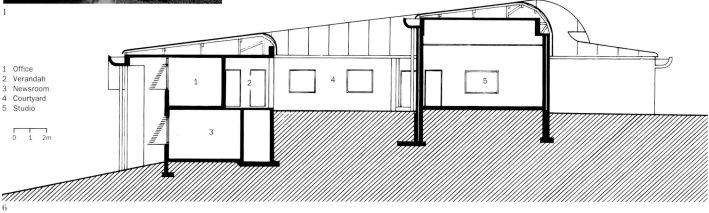

1 Office
2 Verandah
3 Newsroom
4 Courtyard
5 Studio

0   1   2m

Honiara Radio Station, Solomon Islands

Design/Completion 1977/1982
Honiara, Solomon Islands
Australian Government
1,225 square metres
Reinforced concrete, steel roof
Steel roofing, timber storm shutters, glass louvres

The Honiara Radio Station combined elements from the Vila Radio Station with new concepts appropriate for the site. The studios have air-conditioning, which is essential for the acoustics and equipment maintenance, while the offices are naturally ventilated to minimise the use of expensive imported fuel. The site is on a narrow, flat coastal plain, beside a creek that is prone to flooding. The floor is elevated on a pebble stone batter with freestanding concrete columns. The roof is constructed from white corrugated iron, and the walls consist of operable glass louvres. Ventilation is achieved through a palm-filled central courtyard, surrounded by an open verandah. The outer walls have wide overhanging eaves and blue painted timber-framed lattice shutters. These shutters can be bolted in several positions for sun control and act as cyclone protection when fully shut. In its blue, white and grey colouration, its form, and its climate control, the building relates to the typical township character of the islands.

2

3

1

4

1 Detail of sun control and cyclone shutters
2 Elevated building deals with flooding
3 Entrance
4 Courtyard

West Amenities Refit and Control Building

Design/Completion 1978/1981
Garden Island, Sydney, New South Wales
Department of Defence
1,620 square metres
Steel frame with lightweight insulated metal panel system
Polyurethane foam core steel panels (proprietary system)

The prominent location is the nearest point across the water from the parkland at Mrs Macquarie's Chair, a popular harbour viewing spot. Consequently, an unobtrusive building was to be preferred.

There is an extraordinary contrast in scale between the large cranes and the ships at berth and the new building which, with normal clues to its scale, could look overwhelmed. The predominant material in this harbour context is painted steel. The concept, therefore, was the construction of a steel box overscaled by its simplicity with careful attention given to crisp detailing and the resolution of functional issues. Its purpose is for direct management of refits of the ships berthed alongside. Change rooms, toilets and dining facilites are provided for the workers.

The cladding is sandwich panel with steel facings and a polyurethane foam core—the standard product of a large manufacturer. An effort was made to utilise all the design potential of this material, particularly in shaping and detailing. The flush facade was simply pierced as required to satisfy the different functional areas of the building. The lightweight structure allowed the building to be supported as a raft off the existing wharf slab, which is on made ground.

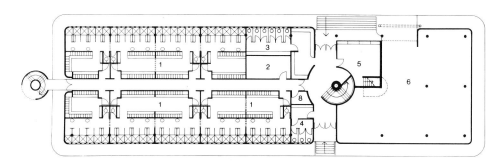

2

1   Shower and change
2   Drying
3   Men's toilet
4   Women's toilet
5   Office
6   Storage
7   Dining
8   Store
9   Plant
10 Lunch

0   2.5   5m

1

3

1   Entrance
2   Level 1 and 2 floor plans
3   Building in its context
4   Facade detail
5   North elevation
6   Contrast in scale

4

5

6

Central Area Lighting, Parliamentary Zone Lake Foreshore Promenade, Urban Design/Landscape Works Project

Design/Completion 1988/1991
Parliamentary Triangle, Canberra, Australian Capital Territory
National Capital Planning Authority
Principal consultant: R.A. Young Civil Engineers
Lighting design: Barry Webb Lighting Design
Landscape architect: Dorrough Britz & Associates
Architects and urban designers: Ancher Mortlock & Woolley
Precast concrete and steel
Off-white, etched precast concrete walls and copings, painted steel and stainless steel light fittings

Ken Woolley was appointed as a consultant on the urban design elements of the Central Area, particularly the axis of the Parliamentary Triangle in Canberra, from a period in the early 1980s. The light fittings and the foreshore are the first elements to be completed.

The special light fitting was developed in order to distinguish the pedestrian areas of the Parliamentary Triangle, which gave rise to its tripartite column and base. When eventually used in all the pedestrian-scale spaces with constant orientation, the fitting will assist visitors to comprehend the oblique angles of roads and buildings encountered away from the central axis.

The edge of Lake Burley Griffin is a particularly important urban design element, long neglected with a temporary "sea wall" and crude landscaping. With increased use of this water edge by pedestrians, a stronger definition was sought. The concept designs developed as part of this project include end pavilions and a water gate on the central axis. To date, however, the formal edge of the lake at the Parliamentary Triangle is the only element of the plan to have been completed. Funding for the implementation of the formal elements needed to delineate the plan seems to have a low priority, and there is a reluctance to commit to the large, tangible, albeit non-utilitarian, items. Thus the foreshore and the lights are the hesitant first steps—secondary linking elements rather than the bastions, pavilions, walls, steps, sculptures, pedestals and fountains which are needed to bring the area to maturity.

1

1 Prototype fitting
2 Promenade at dusk
3 Elevation and site plan

2

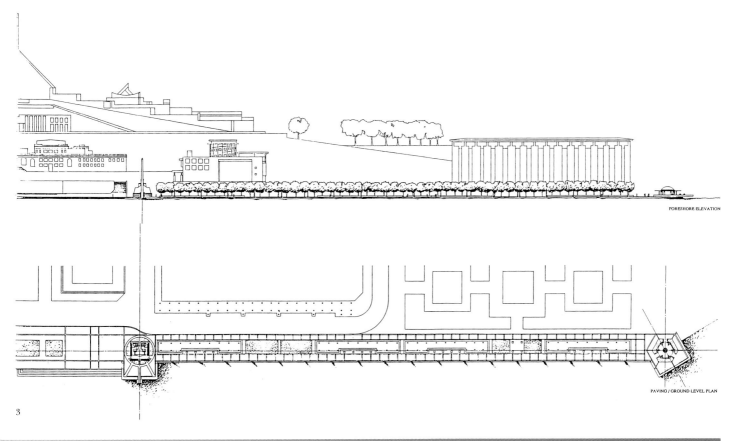

FORESHORE ELEVATION

PAVING / GROUND LEVEL PLAN

3

4   Lake edge
5   Foreshore promenade
6   Site and elevation geometry

4

5

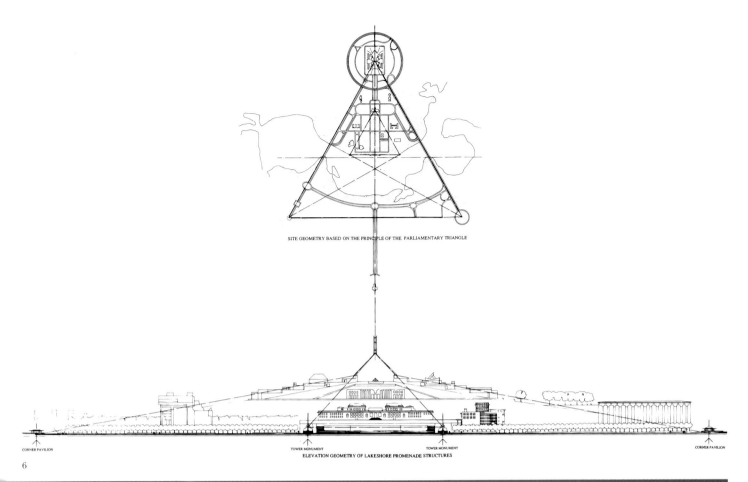

SITE GEOMETRY BASED ON THE PRINCIPLE OF THE PARLIAMENTARY TRIANGLE

ELEVATION GEOMETRY OF LAKESHORE PROMENADE STRUCTURES

CORNER PAVILION   TOWER MONUMENT   TOWER MONUMENT   CORNER PAVILION

6

Linley Cove Housing Development

Design/Completion 1980/1984
Lane Cove, New South Wales
Lend Lease Residential
220 housing units (total area 25,000 square metres)
Winning competition entry
Load-bearing brick, reinforced concrete, timber roofs
Face brick, timber panelling, concrete tile roofs

The site was an abandoned industrial estate with stands of mature native trees and large excavated sandstone terraces, fairly steeply lined along a pleasant stream, with playing fields opposite. The concept set out to provide a rational staged construction and marketing development; building commenced at one end of a loop road allowing residents to progressively occupy completed stages.

Development controls were met by a flexible master plan which could progressively satisfy the imposed residential and parking mix but also respond to the market over several years of development. Vernacular residential construction provided mixed clusters of townhouses, walk-up apartments and overlapping hillside units. The original landscape was enhanced and small-scale roadways and paths avoided the engineered solutions common at the time. The scheme became a model example for housing programs in the 1980s, such as the Better Cities and Amcord programs.

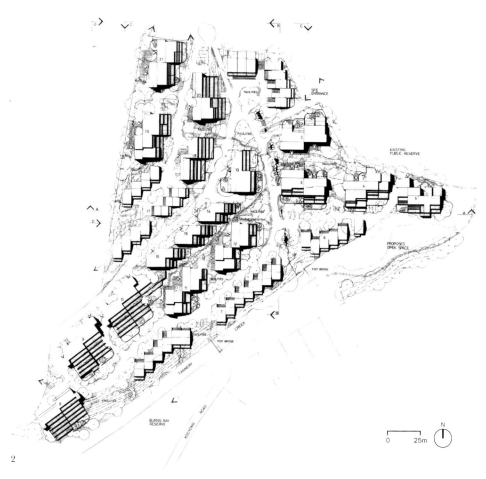

2

1

3

4

5

6

7

8

1 Townhouse group from upper part of site
2 Site plan
3 Group of townhouses with apartments in the background
4 Main roadway and apartments
5 Overlapping apartments on steep hillside
6 Apartments on hillside
7 Townhouses
8 Two-storey apartments adjacent to parkland

Mormon Chapel

Design/Completion 1980/1983
Leura, New South Wales
The Church of Jesus Christ of Latter Day Saints
3,850 square metres
Load-bearing brickwork, steel roof frame
Painted brick, concrete, corrugated iron

The Mormon Church has traditionally chosen the design for each of its local chapels from a set of standardised designs. The chapel at Leura was one of the earliest breaks from this tradition, but was nevertheless required to incorporate the church's familiar symbolism.

The result is a tower with a stylised and tapered finial and low spreading, white, domestic-scale roofs. The prominent hilltop site is typical of locations for traditional churches, so an effort was made to create a building that was recognisable as a church, while eschewing traditional church elements.

Light is the overall theme of the interior, and it is brought in from four sources to play on a volume of white surfaces. Primary sources are the close-mullioned window to the gallery and forecourt, and skylights at the ridge line. A large window recessed into the tower brings light along the surface of the end wall, behind the dais, to pass over the vault of the gallery. The most subtle light enters from a huge half-cylindrical reflector on the west side. Light is reflected up along the roof plane from an opening at the level of the pews, but as the roof extends to the centre of the cylinder, no direct view out is obtained. This cylinder also acts as a somewhat oversized roof gutter.

3

1 Narthex
2 Chapel
3 Cultural hall
4 Font
5 Clerk's office
6 Bishop's office
7 Classrooms

1

2

4

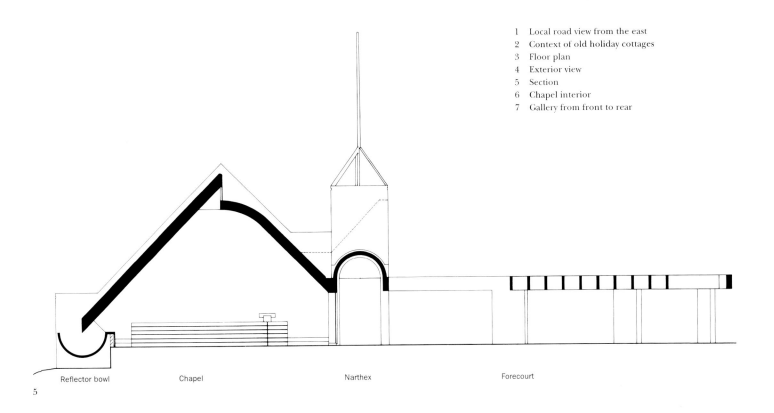

1 Local road view from the east
2 Context of old holiday cottages
3 Floor plan
4 Exterior view
5 Section
6 Chapel interior
7 Gallery from front to rear

Reflector bowl   Chapel   Narthex   Forecourt

5

6

7

Woolley House, Paddington

Design/Completion 1979/1980
Sydney, New South Wales
Ken Woolley
238 square metres
Load-bearing brick, concrete floors
Painted brick walls, waxed brick floors, timber and steel roof

Ken Woolley's Paddington house is an exercise in defensible space, the entrance facade controlling entry and outlook. A public porch at the street looks through an iron grille to the semi-private entrance space. Above, a circular opening in the otherwise blank wall signifies the entrance while allowing the street to be observed. A narrow courtyard lies behind the upper wall that shields the interior from high terrace houses across the street, and from noise. The courtyard, planted in narrow stepped terraces and espaliered camellias to give a *tromp l'oeil* view, provides reflected sun and ventilation. The whole front assembly is a separate facade.

At the rear the house opens out to view and sunshine. Of massive construction (based on standard three-storey apartments but with brick floors), its thermal qualities are excellent.

The rear wall is angled at 45 degrees with its salient turned around a bay. The angle gives more frontage to the lower rooms while at the top it forms a terrace oriented towards a view of Sydney Harbour. The tall brick form at the rear relates to the back of a typical terrace house, complete with traditional but slightly overscaled corbelled chimney.

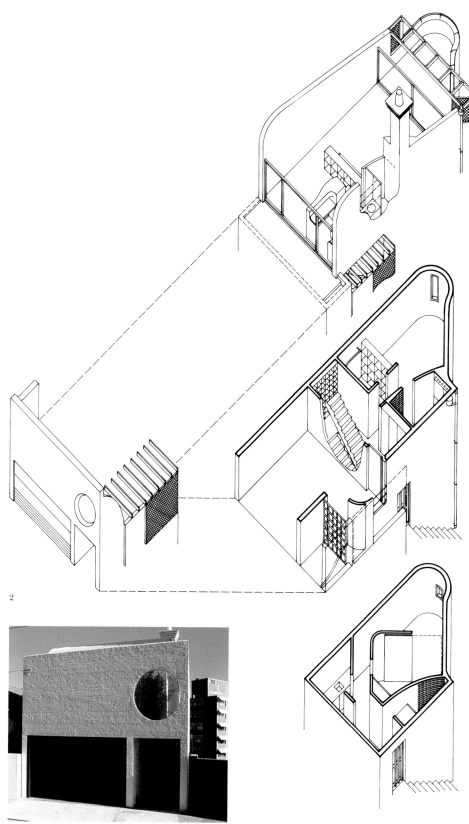

2

3

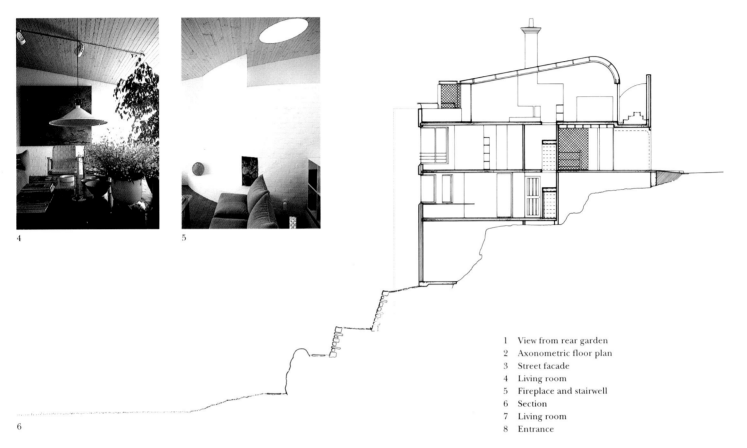

1   View from rear garden
2   Axonometric floor plan
3   Street facade
4   Living room
5   Fireplace and stairwell
6   Section
7   Living room
8   Entrance

Guided Missile Launching System Assembly and Overhaul Building

Design/Completion 1980/1983
Garden Island, Sydney, New South Wales
Department of Housing & Construction on behalf of the
Department of Defence
819 square metres
Steel frame
Lightweight steel insulated panel system

The Guided Missile Launching System (GMLS) building is the second of a series of buildings that extend along the waterfront on the east of Woolloomooloo Bay. The building is used for the installation and servicing of the Harpoon missile armament system of the Royal Australian Navy's frigates. Ships berth below the dockyard crane that lifts the assembly out and lowers it through the opening roof of the GMLS building.

The circular form, which is 23 metres in diameter and 19 metres high, was expressed as a polygon based on the circular internal crane/gantry devised to provide heavy lifting over its entire floor area. The external plant room is linked by large stainless steel ducts. The simple form of the structure and its large sun louvres maintain the necessarily large scale of its setting. The GMLS building is sited adjacent to the West Amenities building and is closely related in form to massive ships and dockyard cranes and equipment.

2

1   Blades of the sun louvres
2   Site plan
3   Prominent in view from Mrs Macquarie's Chair
4   Underside of roof and rotating overhead gantry

1   3

4

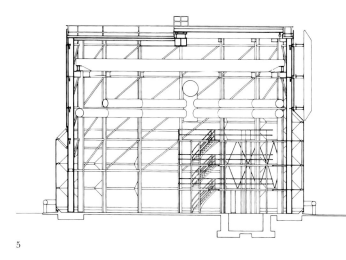

5

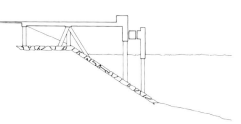

7

8

6

9

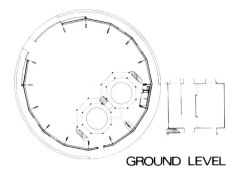

GROUND LEVEL

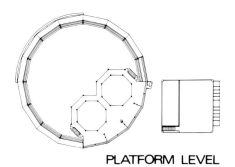

PLATFORM LEVEL

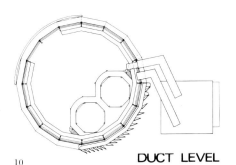

DUCT LEVEL

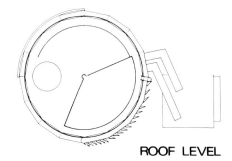

ROOF LEVEL

5   Section
6   Air-conditioning ducts enter from the
    external platform
7   West view
8   Stepped cylinder of the building
9   Detail
10 Floor plans
11 Interior view

10

11

Yarralumla Shores

Design/Completion 1981/1983
Canberra, Australian Capital Territory
B & B Constructions
5,538 square metres (26 houses of 150–350 square metres)
Load-bearing brick, concrete floors
Face brick, aluminium windows, concrete roof tiles

The site adjoins a stretch of parkland on Lake Burley Griffin with views of Black Mountain. It is divided into three townhouse groupings separated by landscaped gardens. Each house is based on a simple L-shaped, two-storey design with extensions to suit site conditions. The aim was to create a degree of individuality and separate building profiles by alternating the size and form of the townhouses. Variety is favoured over continuity but with a deliberate consistency in architectural form and expression.

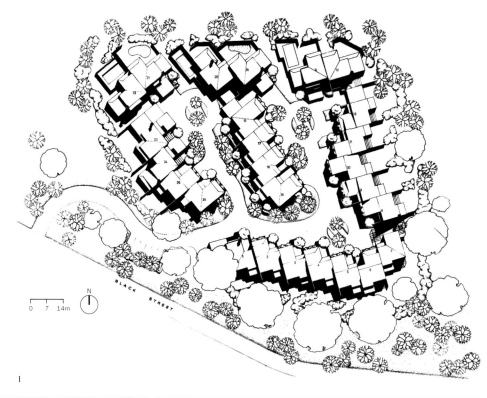

1

2

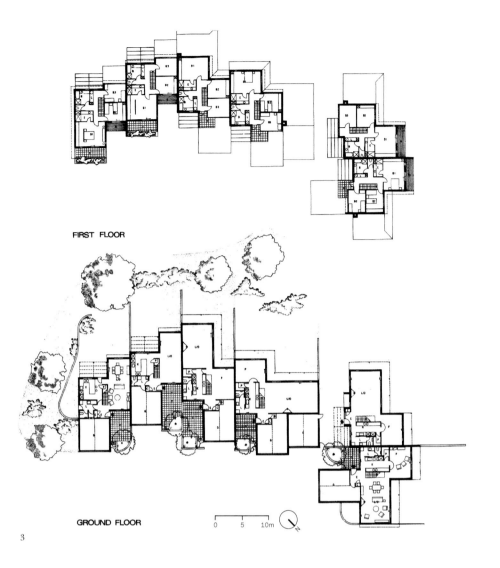

FIRST FLOOR

GROUND FLOOR

0   5   10m

1   Site plan
2   View from Lake Burley Griffin
3   Floor plans
4   Access roadway
5   Cul-de-sac
6   Second cul-de-sac

3

4

5

6

Australian Defence Forces Academy Cadets Mess

Design/Completion 1982/1985
Canberra, Australian Capital Territory
Department of Housing & Construction
6,636 square metres
Joint architects: Department of Housing & Construction
Reinforced concrete frame
Glass block infill panels, glass areas with steel portal frame doors, sandblasted off-form concrete walls, plywood ceilings, timber parquet and carpet floors

The Cadets Mess is the dining and recreational facility for student officers of the Australian Defence Forces Academy (ADFA). A large kitchen serves a staggered plan of various sized dining rooms, leading to terraces overlooking the parade grounds. Upper level lounges overlook the dining areas through open spaces below the glazed roof vaults.

The large square plan areas required a special flat roof system to comply with department policy on metal roof pitches, and uses long concrete intermediate structural gutters serving sections of steel roof decking. Perforated metal screens for sun shading of the quarter-circle roof vaults also provide natural lighting to the internal dining areas.

The building is the main social centre for the resident students and is similar to a university student union, except for the more disciplined atmosphere. It forms one side of the central parade ground where it presents a formality and rhythm, while its entrance side, facing the residential colleges, is much more irregular.

1

1   West entrance
2   Building complex from parade ground
Opposite:
    Detail

2

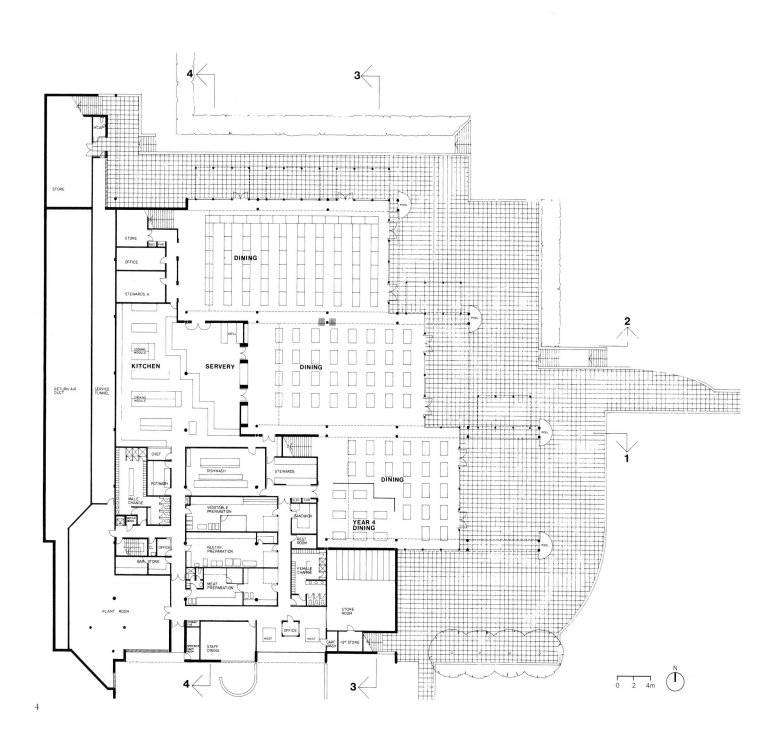

STORE

HCAP

STORE

STORE

OFFICE

STEWARDS A

DINING

POOL

KITCHEN

SERVERY

DINING

POOL

2

RETURN AIR DUCT

SERVICE TUNNEL

COOKING MODULE

COOKING MODULE

GRILL

POOL

1

CHEF

POTWASH

DISHWASH

STEWARDS

DINING

MALE CHANGE

MOTOR ROOM

CL OFFICE

BAR STORE

VEGETABLE PREPARATION

PASTRY PREPARATION

MEAT PREPARATION

ELEC FHR

SANDWICH

REST ROOM

FEMALE CHANGE

YEAR 4 DINING

POOL

PLANT ROOM

HYDRANT

SPRINKLER VALVE ROOM

STAFF DINING

HOIST

OFFICE

HOIST

CART WASH

-12° STORE

STORE ROOM

0 2 4m

N

4

3

4

3

4 Level 1 floor plan
5 Level 2 floor plan

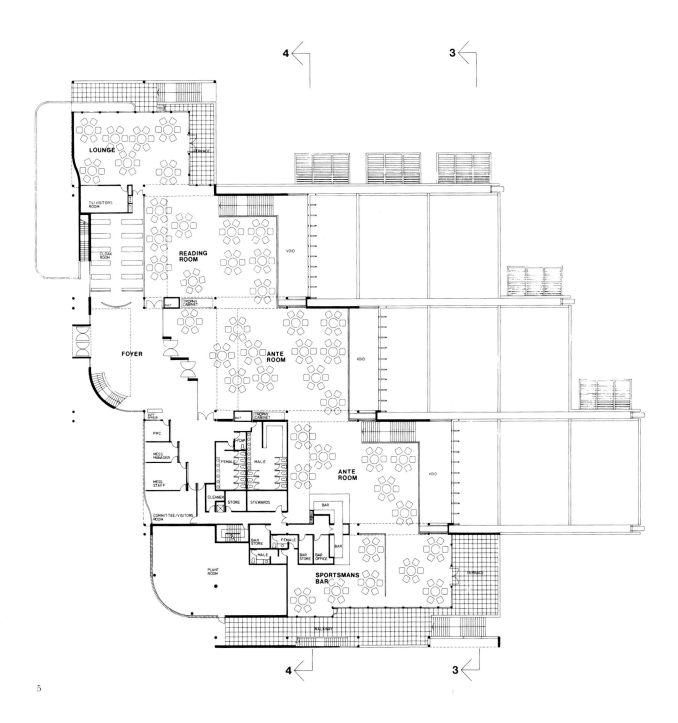

4 ←   **3** ←

LOUNGE

TERRACE

TV/VISITORS ROOM

CLOAK ROOM

READING ROOM

VOID

DUCT   TROPHY CABINET

FOYER

ANTE ROOM

VOID

DUCT   TROPHY CABINET

DUTY OFFICER

PMC

H'CAP

MESS MANAGER

FEMALE   MALE

ANTE ROOM

VOID

MESS STAFF

CLEANER   STORE   STEWARDS

COMMITTEE/VISITORS ROOM

BAR

BAR STORE

FEMALE

BAR

PLANT ROOM

MALE

BAR STORE   BAR OFFICE

SPORTSMANS BAR

TERRACE

WALKWAY

4 ←   **3** ←

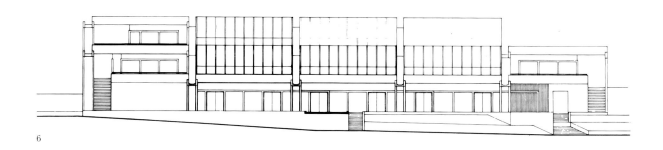

6

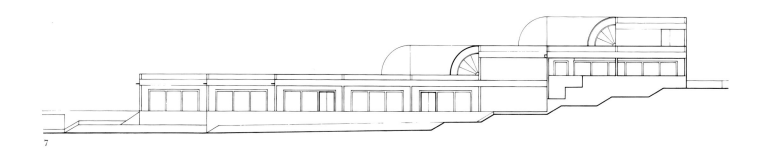

7

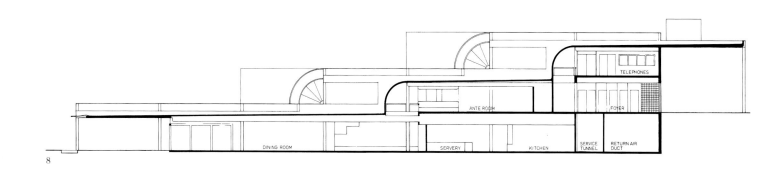

8

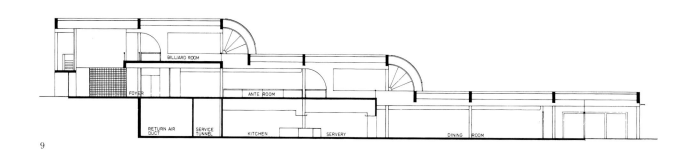

9

10

11

12

13

6   East elevation
7   North elevation
8   Section 1
9   Section 2
10   Lounge area showing roof arc
11   Dining area showing the roof and second level
12   Parade ground elevation
13   Dining area

Woolley House, Palm Beach

Design/Completion 1985/1986
Palm Beach, New South Wales
Ken Woolley
150 square metres
Timber frame
Tallowwood weatherboard, celery-top pine joinery, corrugated steel roof,
copper gutters and details, unpainted soft fibreboard wall linings

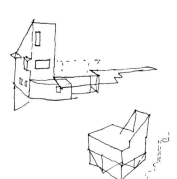

Located next to a waterfall in a sheltered rainforest gully 150 metres from the ocean beach, this house is designed like a small wooden tower and climbs the cliff as a staircase, giving access to decks and spectacular views. The building sits on a precarious slope with its foundations rock-bolted to the sandstone escarpment. The difficulties of the site and the mild microclimate of the area led to the decision to construct the house completely from timber.

The structure is in three vertical layers with a braced and latticed base. The first floor consists of bedrooms with relatively small windows and is clad with hardwood weatherboards. The second level forms a single living area with continuous windows on three sides. Above that is a loft and staircase leading to a narrow bridge to the top of the cliff. The casement windows are designed to catch the breeze; larger openings have sliding screened doors to timber decks at the rear and side. Screened vent panels flap down between the rafters.

Three different timber deck areas run behind and beside the house, along the cliff face. One acts as a sheltered courtyard, the next is a covered outdoor room and the most remote is open to the sun. These are the reverse of the typical verandahs usually seen along the outer edges of houses on steep sites. There are many similarities between this house and the 1962 house at Mosman.

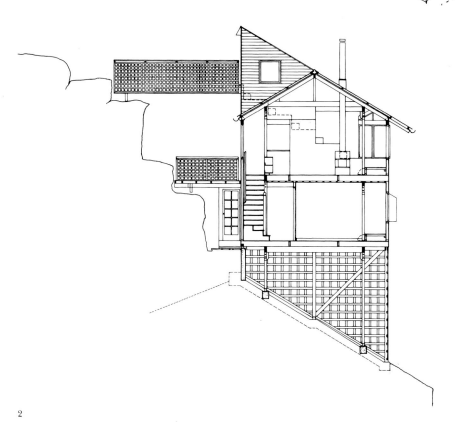

2

1

3

1 Bedroom hallway
2 Section
3 North elevation
4 Living room from loft stair
5 Waterfall side

4

5

6   Open deck
7   Covered "sala" and rear courtyard deck
8   Living room

6

7

8

Queenscliff Surf Pavilion

Design/Completion 1982/1983
Sydney, New South Wales
Brian Pettit, Whiteholme/Manly Council
1,350 square metres
Brick, concrete
Rendered and painted brick, concrete, laminated timber, copper roof

The Queenscliff Surf Pavilion replaced an earlier brick building that had deteriorated badly from exposure to sea, wind and sand. The most northern of three surf pavilions along Manly Beach, it is situated at the point where Manly Lagoon discharges into the sea across the beach in times of flood. It has a community hall (shared with the surf club), change rooms, public toilets, clubrooms, an observation room and first aid room. There is also an administration area, a caretaker's flat and surfing goods stores. The tower acts as a reference point, clock tower and observation platform for the lifesavers.

The building is supported on deep piles behind the existing sandstone sea wall, which is often scoured by flooding and high tides. The concept is that of an isolated pavilion set on the edge of the sand, with a background of houses and flats, and flanked by cliffs, sand and sea. It is in context with surrounding natural forms and surfaces and in contrast to the residential area.

1   Screen colonnade looking to ocean
2   Site plan
3   Pavilion viewed from the beach
4   Wave-form roof seen from the bridge

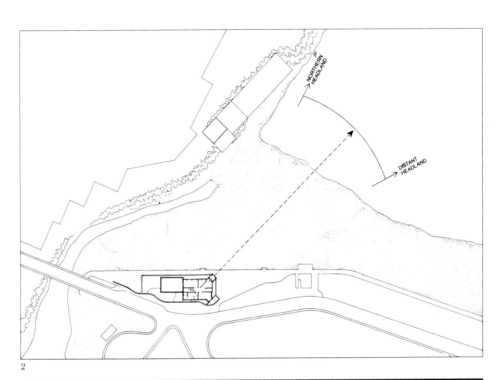

2

3

1

4

93 George Street, Parramatta

Design/Completion 1984/1986
Parramatta, New South Wales
Pettit/Whiteholme, State Superannuation Board
14,305 square metres
Concrete frame
Face brickwork, glass curtain walls to courtyard, standard office finishes

The building set out to be an ordinary office building with three levels of car parking, two of them above ground, and five levels of office space above this, with a large central terraced courtyard. Council parking requirements and restrictions on deep underground parking due to the watertable dictated above-ground parking floors, which presented a difficult civic design problem for the facades. This was addressed by making the facade very thick, with deep window openings, with the result that the parking floor is hard to distinguish from the offices above.

Flexibility of floor planning was the major functional requirement, and led to the adoption of a bilateral floor plan. The central core and foyer divide the floors, permitting independent open-planned office spaces on each side. Multiple reflections in the courtyard create an illusion of space and a complex, interesting outlook from what would otherwise be an excessively narrow and deep office space. The stepped terraces of the courtyard also provide different rentable floor areas at each level.

2

1

3

4

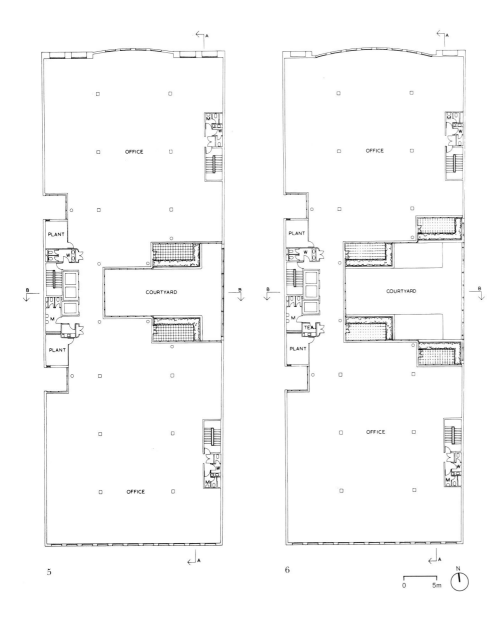

7

1   Multiple reflections
2   Courtyard balcony terraces
3   Brick facade detail
4   Courtyard behind the boundary wall
5   Level 4 and 5 floor plan
6   Level 6 and 7 floor plan
7   Street elevation
8   Internal courtyard as office outlook
9   Courtyard reflections
10 Outlook to the city

5

6

0   5m

N

8

9

10

Commonwealth Law Courts

Design/Completion 1984/1987
Parramatta, New South Wales
Australian Construction Services, Attorney General's Department
12,330 square metres
Reinforced concrete frame, steel roof
Precast concrete, sandstone and trachyte cladding, copper and bronze
detailing

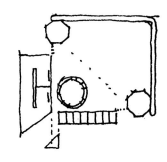

This is a freestanding building on part of a large site that contains new government offices. A public square separates the rather overbearing glass-walled offices from the Commonwealth Law Courts, which were designed in masonry to complement the older civic buildings of Parramatta in character, materials and scale.

The building's main function is to house the Family Court, a Federal Court, and Administrative Appeals Tribunal hearing rooms. The plan characteristics arise from the separate circulation of the public and the judges, who enter on opposite sides of the building and meet only in the courtrooms. With the building being on a corner of a square site, these two entrances naturally move to diagonally opposite corners. This sets up a diagonal interface for the internal circulation and locates the public entrance at the closest point to the central area of Parramatta where it can be related to the old tower of the State Courthouse.

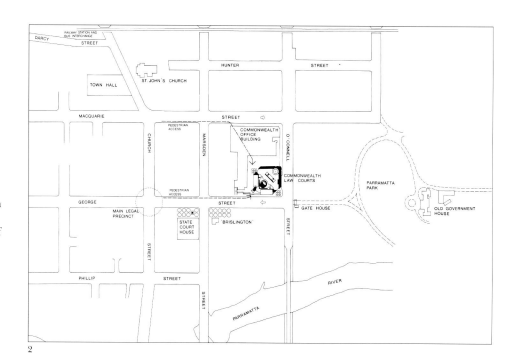

2

1   Lift tower with clock from George Street
2   Locality plan
3   Western elevation with judges' entrance
4   Old Government House, Gate House and
    Law Courts
5   Clock tower detail
6   Public entrance

1

3

4

5

6

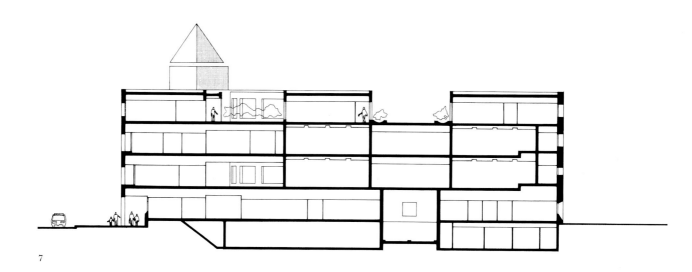

7

8

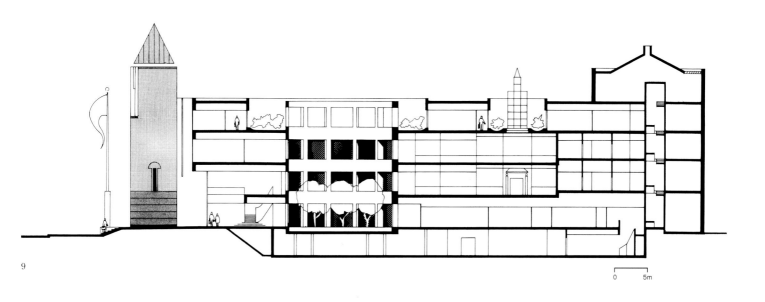

9

0   5m

10

11

12

13

14

7   Cross-section
8   Detail of ground floor windows
9   Diagonal section
10   Light wells looking up to roof lanterns
11   Courtroom doorways and circulation space
12   Courtroom
13   Central courtyard
14   Judges' roof garden with lanterns

The Anchorage

Design/Completion 1982/1985
Tweed Heads, New South Wales
Lend Lease Residential
4,720 square metres (Stage 1)
Brick, timber, concrete floors
Plaster, render, timber lattice, concrete roof tiles

The site is in an extraordinarily beautiful landscape: lush river valleys with a backdrop of volcanic mountain forms, covered in rainforest. The residential development was confined to an area which hosted the remaining stand of trees on an island in the Tweed River. The development is conceived as a harbour with beaches and quaysides, and is approached across a bridge.

The harbour was created by moving sand and profiling the building areas and beaches as required, so that the site would suit the most desirable housing rather than the reverse. In one section, an artificial pyramidal hill was created ready for a four-sided, terraced overlap housing group similar to the Penthouses in Sydney. The waterway was designed and tested in a hydraulics laboratory to ensure water quality would be maintained by tidal circulation.

The first stage comprises a variety of waterfront and hinterland housing: ten townhouses, eight garden/loft apartments and four luxury units. Construction is fairly conventional, with considerable care and attention given to the detailing of the primary timber elements.

1   Waterfront house
2   Site plan
3   Waterfront house with timber deck promenade
Opposite:
    Balcony view from upper apartment

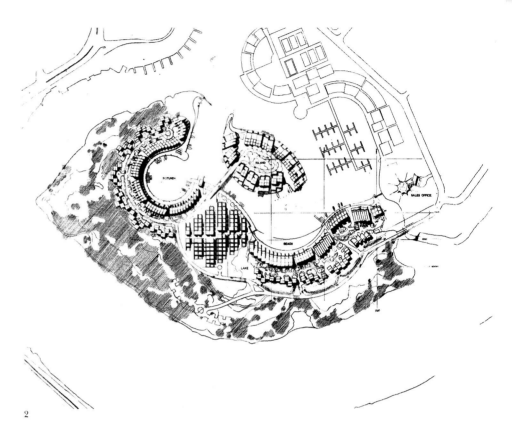

2

1

3

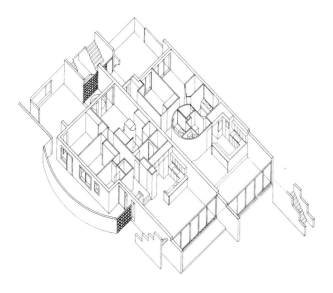

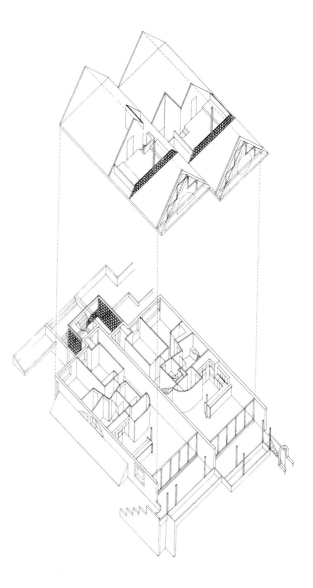

5

6

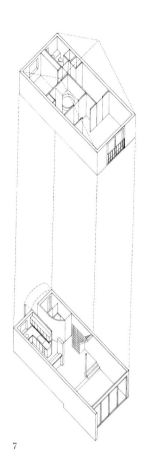
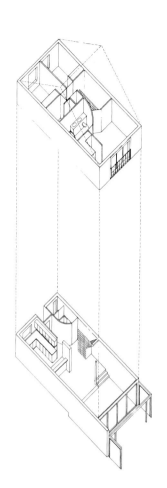
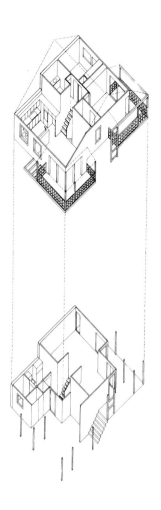

7

8

Park Hyatt Hotel

Design/Completion 1986/1990
Circular Quay, Sydney, New South Wales
CRI Limited
18,168 square metres
Reinforced concrete frame
Precast concrete, sandstone, ochre-coloured render, metalwork

In 1986 the New South Wales Government conducted a design tender competition for offers to lease this waterfront site at Campbells Cove, which was then occupied by industrial and marine service buildings. The site is important, as it forms the western component of a gateway to Circular Quay, with the Opera House serving the matching function on the eastern side.

The shape of the site follows the small cove and gives rise to the idea of a sinuous form with all rooms facing out onto the harbour, most looking across to the Opera House. The strength of this shape assists the relationship with the large-scale elements of the adjoining Harbour Bridge and park.

To relate to the finer scale and texture of the historic waterfront neighbourhood of the Rocks, the hotel facades are composed of a rhythmic repetition of emphasised double bays and are divided horizontally into base, middle floors and set-back loggias at roof level. Within these divisions, variations of balconies, rooflines and window divisions add interest.

1   Hotel entrance with Opera House in background
2   Campbells Cove from the overseas terminal
3   Waterfront promenade
Opposite:
    The Rocks with city behind

2

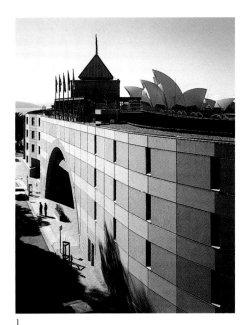

1

3

5

6

5   Elevation
6   Waterfront restaurants and lobbies

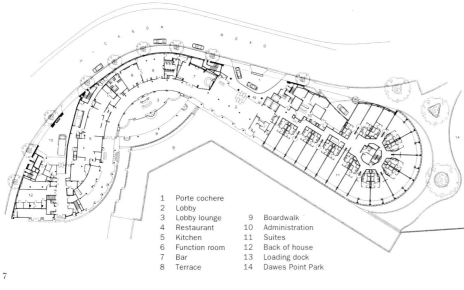

1	Porte cochere		
2	Lobby		
3	Lobby lounge	9	Boardwalk
4	Restaurant	10	Administration
5	Kitchen	11	Suites
6	Function room	12	Back of house
7	Bar	13	Loading dock
8	Terrace	14	Dawes Point Park

7

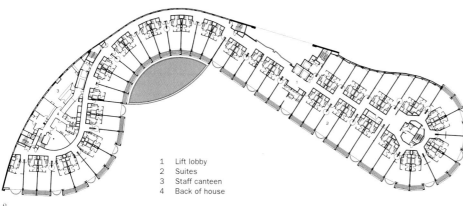

1	Lift lobby
2	Suites
3	Staff canteen
4	Back of house

8

9

10

Australian Pavilion, Expo 88

Design/Completion 1986/1988
Brisbane, Queensland
Department of Housing & Construction
4,749 square metres
Steel frame with lightweight floors and cladding
Steel, timber, corrugated steel, fibre cement

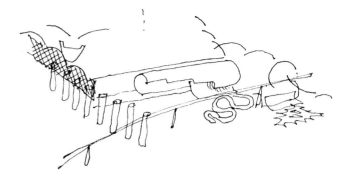

As the host government pavilion, the Australian Pavilion at Expo 88 was designed to be unique, exciting and memorable. The concept set out to depart from the tendency to make heroic architectural statements at Expos, and instead opted for an arrangement of architectural symbols composed in such a way as to reject any idea of permanency. As well as being an enclosure for entertainment, information and exhibitions, the building itself reflected images of Australia and the themes of leisure and technology. It contained a theatre of illusion, a general exhibit hall and large VIP entertainment areas.

The design was not a formal entity but rather a collage of architectural devices drawn from aspects of the Australian landscape. For example, the north elevation is made from multiple layers of lattice and rows of columns, producing shadow effects reminiscent of a forest, while on the west, the rolled corrugated iron, with its connotations of bush architecture, is formed into cylinders like breaking waves.

As a painted building, the design was elaborated with a profusion of brilliant colours, prepared by George Freedman. The large sign sculptures announcing Australia were created by Ken Done, who also provided the staff uniforms and souvenirs.

The pavilion was designed to exist only for the six-month period of Expo 88. It was demolished immediately afterwards, and this literal de-construction process can be identified in the architectural organisation of the design.

1

2

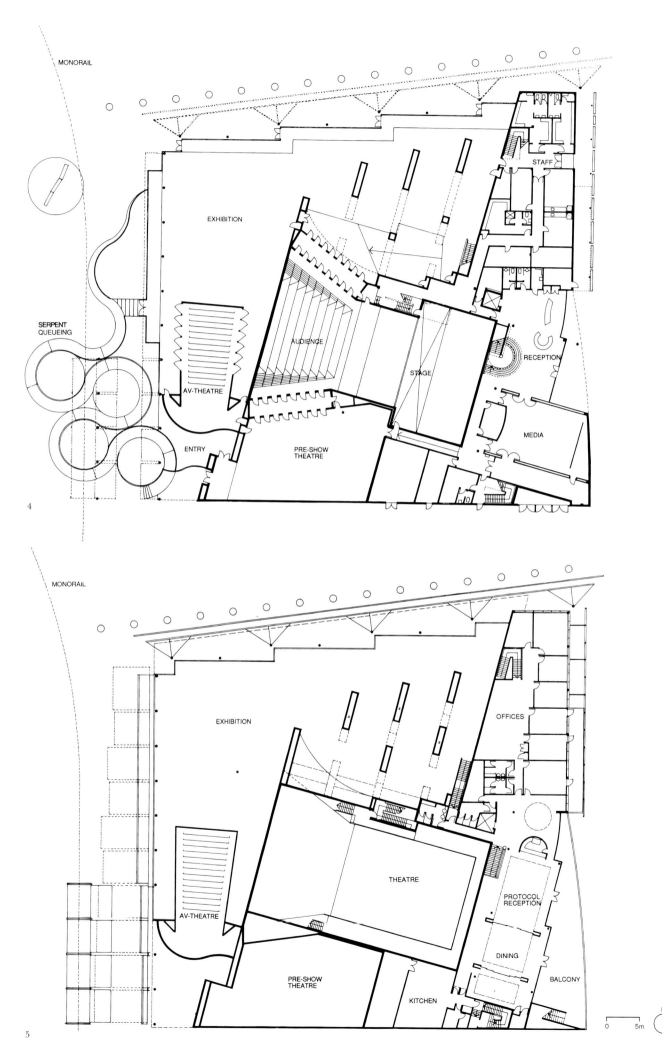

MONORAIL

EXHIBITION

STAFF

SERPENT
QUEUEING

AUDIENCE

STAGE

RECEPTION

AV-THEATRE

MEDIA

ENTRY

PRE-SHOW
THEATRE

4

MONORAIL

EXHIBITION

OFFICES

AV-THEATRE

THEATRE

PROTOCOL
RECEPTION

PRE-SHOW
THEATRE

DINING

BALCONY

KITCHEN

0   5m

N

5

6

7

8

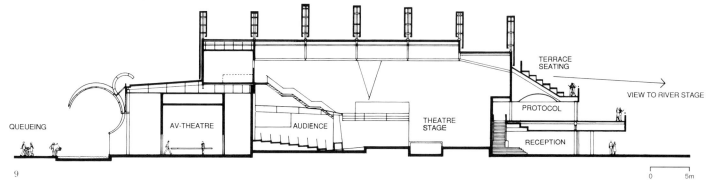

QUEUEING   AV-THEATRE   AUDIENCE   THEATRE STAGE   TERRACE SEATING   VIEW TO RIVER STAGE   PROTOCOL   RECEPTION

9

0   5m

11

9   Section
10&11   Wave forms sheltering queue space for
         theatres
12   Eastern VIP entrance at night
13   Reception lounge
14   Reception, lounge and dining area

10   12

13

14

15

The Australian Hellenic War Memorial

Design/Completion 1986/1987
Anzac Parade, Canberra, Australian Capital Territory
National Capital Planning Authority
1,054 square metres
Concrete
Off-form concrete, steel, slate, bronze, mosaic tile
Winning competition entry

The Australian Hellenic Memorial was the subject of a limited competition for architects and sculptors conducted by the National Capital Planning Authority in 1986. Prepared by Ken Woolley, the statement of design was so well regarded by the Greek-Australian community that it was engraved in a stone on the monument itself.

As an urban design element, the scale and siting of the massive, apparently part-buried column is directed at the enormous scale of the Anzac Parade vista from the Australian War Memorial axis. Here the Hellenic Campaign memorial forms the leading architectural element in a landscape composition.

The executed work is identical to the competition entry, apart from the incision of a Greek cross in the "ruined" ancient column and the use of riveted steel columns from a wrecked building in Sydney instead of the armour plate originally proposed. As intended, this steelwork, from a building of the World War II period, was further damaged by gunfire, provided by courtesy of the Australian Army. Wally Barda developed the design concept and Mary Hall made the mosaic pavement, which is a map of the Aegean region.

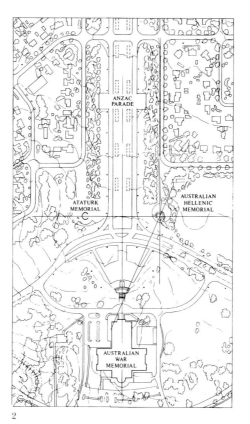

2

3

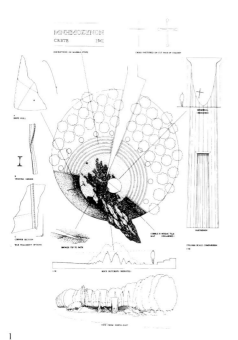

1

4

1   Memorial details
2   Site plan
3   View from the top of Anzac Parade
4   The doric column, buried and overscaled
5   Rocks representing mountain terrain
6   Amphitheatre

5

6

"The Arc" Glasshouses

Design/Completion 1985/1987
Sydney, New South Wales
Royal Botanic Gardens, Sydney
1,358 square metres
Stainless steel, concrete, glass
Sandblasted concrete block, concrete, stainless steel, laminated glass

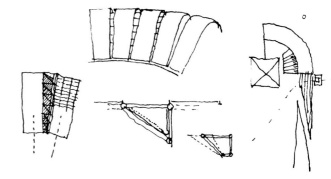

Part of the beauty of traditional glasshouses is the way that flat glass sheets are adapted to complex shapes and curves. The formal geometry of the design, which is curved in both plan and section, is achieved using a series of parallel-sided sections that are curved only in profile, allowing all glass in these sections to be of uniform size. To make up the curve, wedge-shaped segments are inserted between the main sections; these consist of fine tubular stainless steel trusses with triangular glazing between their members.

The stainless steel structure is essentially a number of radiating wedge-shaped trusses separated by tubular purlins that support the main glass sections. The glazing system utilises sophisticated silicone technology, eliminating conventional glazing bars and allowing the laminated glass to contribute to the structure itself. Corrosion-prone materials are eliminated and a low-maintenance, easily cleaned building is the result. In Sydney's warm climate, glasshouses are used to protect tropical plants from drying out, but must be cooled in summer. The glass therefore has a shade factor and a form of air-conditioning is required. The profile of the glasshouse in section is that of a tree canopy, allowing a typical arrangement of rainforest specimens.

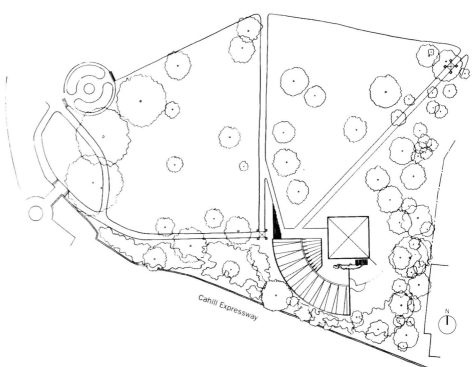

Cahill Expressway

1

1   Site plan
2   Glasshouse at dusk with city in the background
Opposite:
     "The Arc" with pyramid glasshouse in the background

2

4   Section
5   Interior of glasshouse showing tiered planting
6   Plan
7   Looking south-west with pyramid

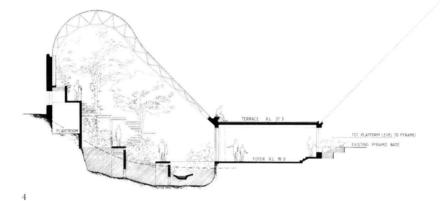

4

5

6

7

ABC Radio and Orchestra Centre

Design/Completion 1986/1990
Ultimo, Sydney, New South Wales
Australian Broadcasting Corporation
35,000 square metres
Reinforced concrete, precast concrete, curtain wall facades, lightweight steel, panel structures to atrium
Precast concrete, steel-framed glazed south lights, lightweight metal panels, carpet and granite floors, perforated metal ceilings; rehearsal/performance/ recording hall and large studios double sound-isolated on rubber bearings with plasterboard, wall linings and timber floors

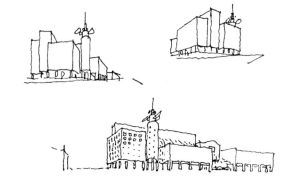

This project is a radio studio and orchestra building with support facilities consisting of office areas, storage, workshops, deliveries, and staff amenities. The principal organising feature of the design is the circulation system that has to deal with extensive horizontal and vertical movements.

An important function of the building was to bring together a number of dispersed radio stations and establish a corporate identity without losing the sense of individuality and elan of the smaller-scale units. The corporation was particularly concerned that a typical multi-storey office building would only enable staff to meet in a ground floor lift lobby, and the expression of individual components would be overwhelmed by a monolithic building.

The resulting proposal was based on the metaphor of a township. The corporation is the "town" as a whole with a central place, a main street and public buildings from which local roads serve particular neighbourhoods. To reach and move between various areas it is necessary to move through the common space. Thus all circulation is within the atrium and all common uses, such as the library, master control, staff lounge and concert hall, open from it. The various radio stations and the head office are also accessed from it.

1

1 Elevation detail
2 View from Harris Street
Oppostie:
    Detail of stair tower and atrium

2

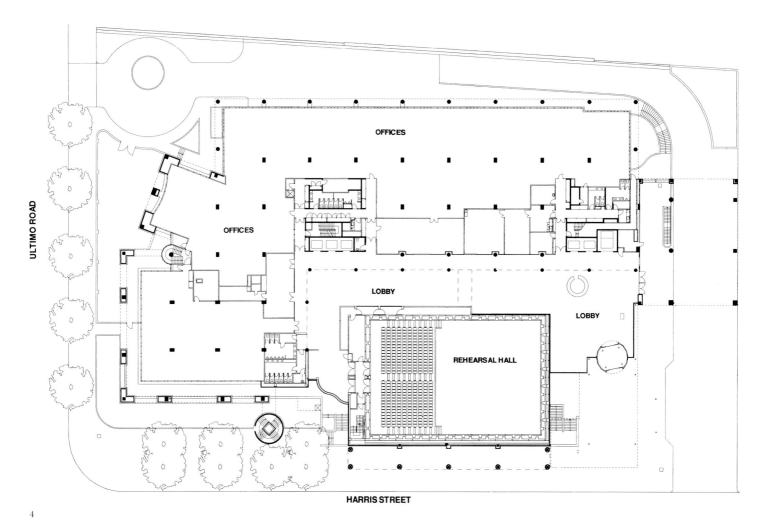

ULTIMO ROAD

OFFICES

OFFICES

LOBBY

LOBBY

REHEARSAL HALL

HARRIS STREET

4

N

OFFICES

STUDIOS

STUDIOS

STUDIOS

STUDIOS

STUDIOS

OFFICES

STUDIOS

OFFICES

STUDIOS

STUDIOS

OFFICES

OFFICES

STUDIOS

TERRACE

5

156   ABC Radio and Orchestra Centre

6

4   Ground floor plan
5   Upper floor plan
6   Gallery access level with southlight glazing
7   Staff lounge and terrace above orchestra hall

7

8

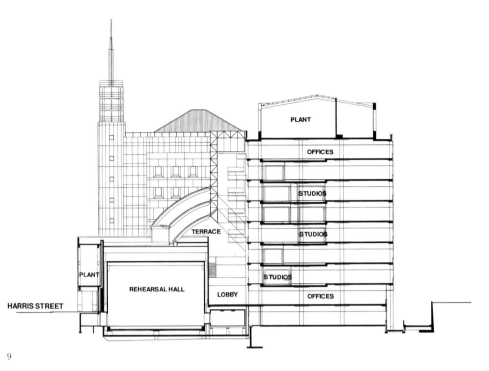

9

PLANT

OFFICES

STUDIOS

STUDIOS

TERRACE

STUDIOS

PLANT

REHEARSAL HALL

LOBBY

OFFICES

HARRIS STREET

10

8 Atrium
9 Section 1
10 Interior of radio studio
11 Section 2
12 Orchestra hall

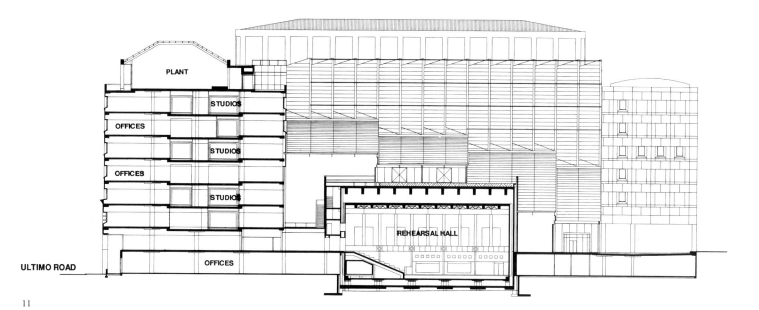

11

12

13

13   Communication stairs
Opposite:
    Atrium looking towards south glazing

Children's Medical Research Institute

Design/Completion 1991/1992
Westmead, New South Wales
Children's Medical Research Institute
5,000 square metres
Concrete frame with steel external columns and roof structure
Painted steelwork, steel-faced sandwich panels, corrugated steel roof,
aluminium windows, adjustable louvres

The Children's Medical Research Institute (CMRI) is a research and administrative facility with two levels of accommodation providing research laboratories, support laboratories, administration and directorate areas, and library, seminar and building services.

The project involved innovative planning of laboratories and shared research facilities. The plan form has a central core of support areas surrounded by groups of four laboratories in a pinwheel configuration. A perimeter corridor between the two areas provides working access to the support facilities and holding areas as well as compartmentalising the plan to meet safety regulations.

A central atrium and stair link all the common elements and provide a point of contact for all users and a means of orientation. All laboratory windows have automatic sun control louvres which can provide special dim-out conditions when required.

The CMRI is functionally and financially independent from the Children's Hospital although they retain many close research links. The new building reflects this independence, yet has provisions for future physical links to the Children's Hospital.

1

1   Entrance
2   Main reception area
Opposite:
    Central stairwell

2

4 Laboratory
5 Ground floor plan
6 First floor plan
7 Section
8 Conference room

4

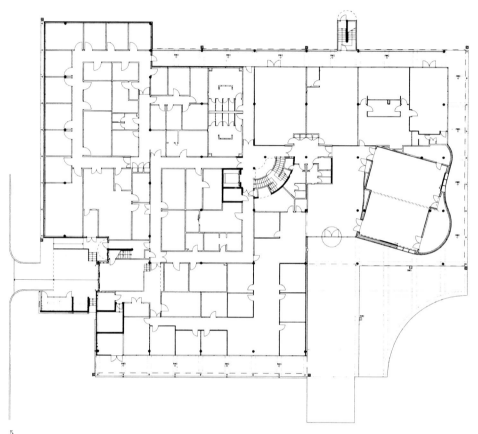

5

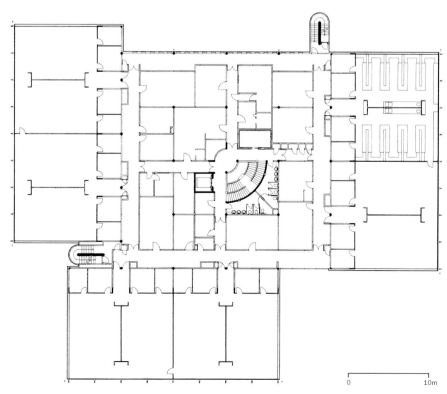

6

0   10m

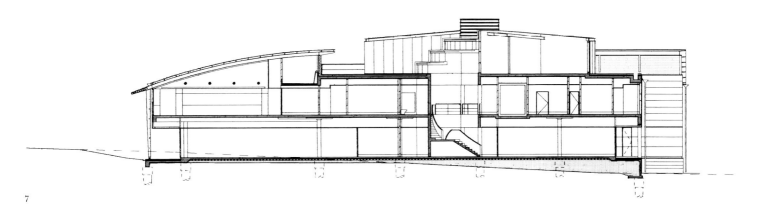

7

8

Walsh Bay

Design/Completion 1989 (project)
Sydney, New South Wales
CRI Limited
53,000 square metres
Existing hardwood structure
Weatherboards, plasterboard interiors, stainless steel and steel detailing

This was the first scheme for the Walsh Bay redevelopment tender which was awarded to CRI in 1989; Ancher Mortlock & Woolley were architects for the three finger wharves (one was already refurbished for the Sydney Theatre Company), the brick-faced shore sheds and the western Towns Place site. Although documentation proceeded, the project was abandoned during the financial recession of the early 1990s.

The Permanent Conservation Order and official Development Guidelines which came into effect in 1989 were drafted to describe exactly the solution to the constraints as presented by this proposal. The policy was to preserve the timber wharf and shore shed structures, replace the timber piles with concrete and, through adaptive reuse as apartments and a hotel, develop the fenestration within the discipline of the main heavy hardwood frame and the overall chequerboard patterns of openings and boarded panels.

A similar scheme was presented by the same team when the tendering process was reactivated in 1996, enhanced by options for a concert hall and a theatre and complying with the conservation order and guidelines. However, because of its realistic emphasis on piling and conservation costs, based on the experience of the earlier scheme, the proposal was not adopted. A different developer won the tender but later succeeded in getting approval to demolish one of the piers and all of the shore sheds, despite the conservation orders.

1

2

1   Montage of Walsh Bay and the city beyond
2   Walsh Bay model: 1989 scheme
3   Ground floor plan and east elevation
4&5   Walsh Bay model: 1989 scheme

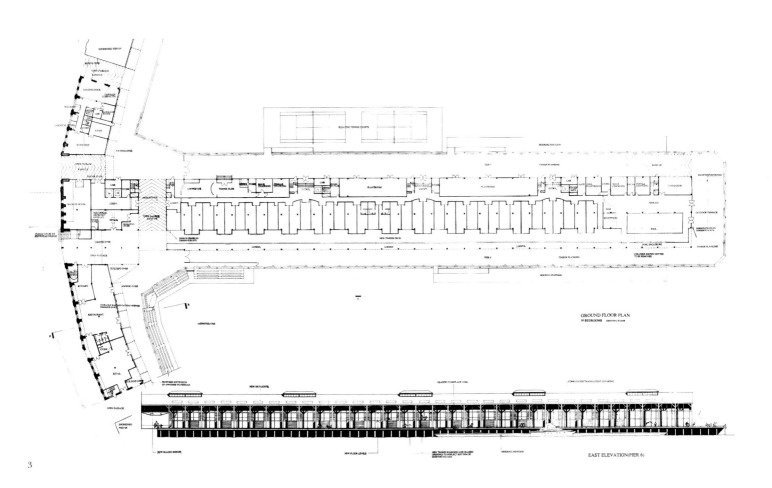

GROUND FLOOR PLAN

36 BEDROOMS   EXISTING FLOOR

EAST ELEVATION (PIER 6)

3

4

5

State Library of Victoria

Design/Completion 1985 (library and museum); 1989 (library only)/2003
Melbourne, Victoria
Government of Victoria, Office of Major Projects
39,000 square metres (net usable area)
Reinforced concrete, steel
Precast concrete, bluestone, sandstone, glazed skylights,
bronze and marble finishes
Winning competition entry

The project was the result of a design competition for the Victorian State Library and Museum, which the architects won in 1986. Expansion onto the adjoining site was subsequently abandoned, and the current project is for the redevelopment of the library only, including the refurbishment, adaptive reuse and restoration of heritage buildings and the construction of new infill buildings and courtyards. Technical requirements include the integration of services such as document retrieval systems and multimedia computer facilities within heritage buildings. Progress is dependent on the relocation of the Museum of Victoria.

Restoration and adaptive reuse involves 13 adjoining buildings erected between 1865 and 1965. These old buildings form one of the most important heritage groups in Australia. Of particular significance is the domed reading room, based on the reading room at the British Museum, which was the largest concrete dome in the world at the time of its construction in 1911. It is an interesting blend of Classical and Federation style with modern engineering detail and simplified, early modern architectural elements. The project includes restoration of the glass rooflights to the dome and other significant spaces, completion of two more toplit courtyards and refurbishment of McCoy Hall.

New work consists of three new infill buildings and four new infills in the courtyards. The new infill buildings complete the street facades and reflect the various periods of construction, serving to tie together the scale, materials and detail.

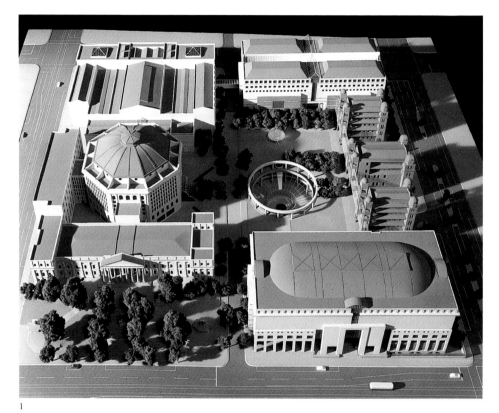

1   Model of the original competition winning scheme
2   Corner of La Trobe and Russell Streets looking at the south-east infill, north-east infill and new administration building
3   The Pitt Building (administration) from La Trobe Street

3

4 Level 2 floor plan
5 Level 3 floor plan
6 The Trescowthick Centre (main reference area)
7 Entry to the main reference area from the west link
8 North-west courtyard atrium showing the external walls
of Queen Hall (bluestone) and the dome library

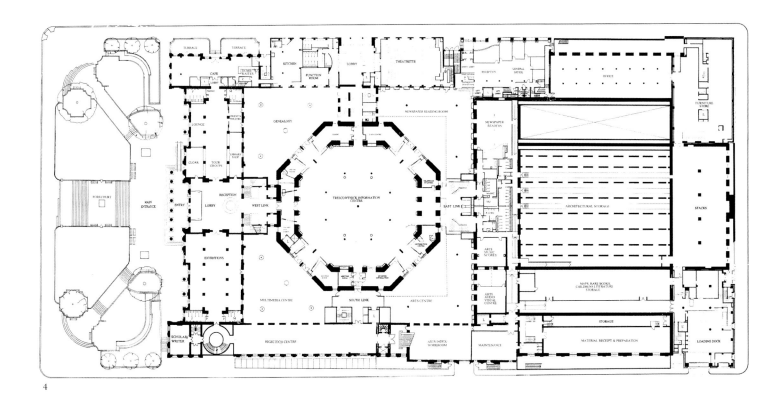

4

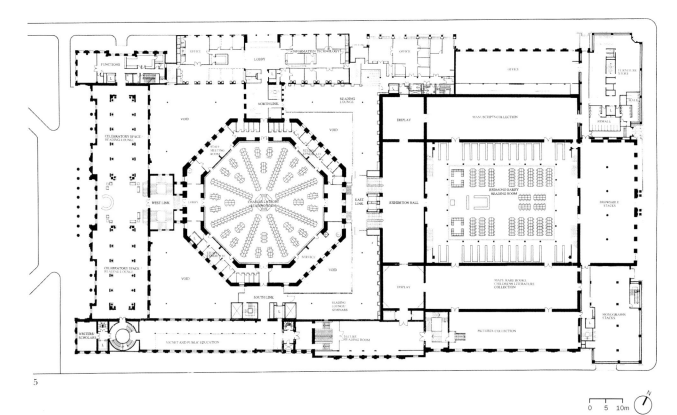

5

6

7

8

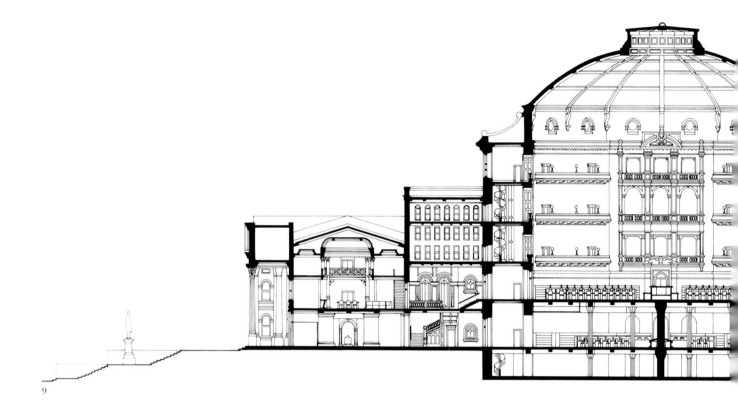

9

10

11

9   Long section through Queens Hall and dome,
    and McCoy Hall
10 From La Trobe Street showing north-east infill
    and the Pitt Building
11 La Trobe theatrette
12 North-east courtyard newspaper reading room
13 North-east courtyard mezzanine

12

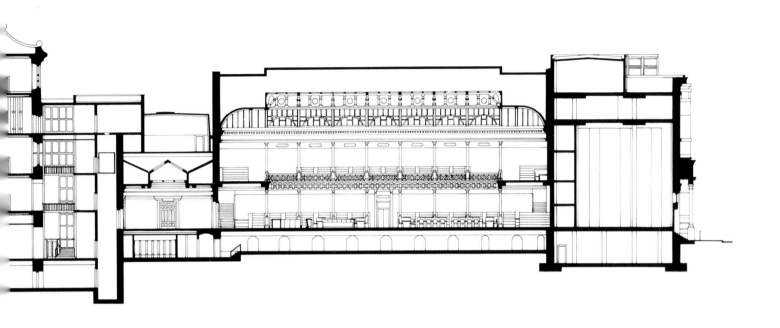

Pettit Weekender

Design/Completion 1985/1989
Scotland Island, New South Wales
Brian Pettit
376 square metres
Timber frame
Timber, corrugated steel, grey-stained weatherboard

This house is on an island in the middle of Pittwater, close to the Palm Beach peninsula, with access only by boat. The sites are very narrow and wedge-shaped, and a long jetty and slipway project these lines far out into the water. From this emerged the idea of carrying a reminder of the diverging boundaries through the house itself. Opportunities are taken to shift the house elements, oscillating from one alignment to the other. The small timber pavilions adopt the scale of small fishermen's huts and boatsheds, with emphasis on the casual and accidental. Roofs are all corrugated steel, walls are grey-stained weatherboard and floors are tile and carpet. Interior walls are clear finished timber. Originally designed as a weekender, the house later became the owner's principal residence.

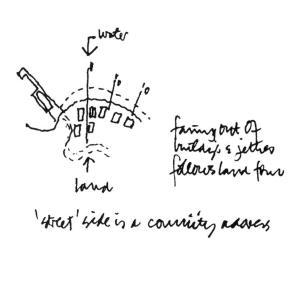

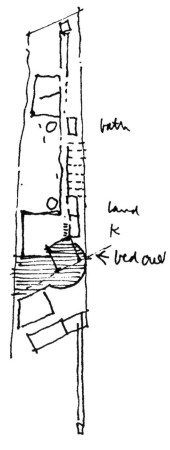

1   Jetty from the house terrace
2   Long jetty
3   Boatshed and small beach
4   Living room with stairs to bedroom
5   Timber stairs and roof structure

1

2

3

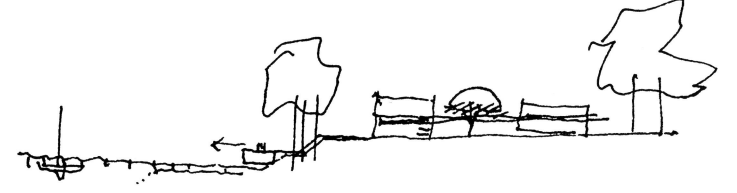

4

5

Waterfront House

Design/Completion 1990/1991
Vaucluse, New South Wales
1,000 square metres
Brick, concrete
Coloured render; sandstone; copper roof; timber windows;
sandstone, carpet and timber floors

The requirement was for a large private house on two amalgamated sites of quite awkward shape with a frontage to a small beach on Sydney Harbour. A tennis court was required on the other side. The design spreads the accommodation over three storeys of generous rooms with external terraces and a waterfront swimming pool. Finishes are of a high standard with comprehensive detail.

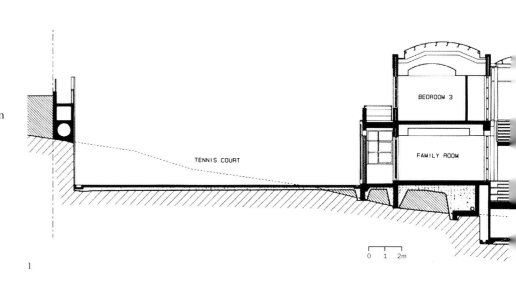

1

2

3

4

1 Section
2 Terraces and pool
3 Side gallery and privacy screening
4 Guest bedroom terrace
5 View from guest bedroom terrace overlooking
   crescent
6 Living room terrace
7 Side gallery
8 Swimming pool overlooking Sydney Harbour

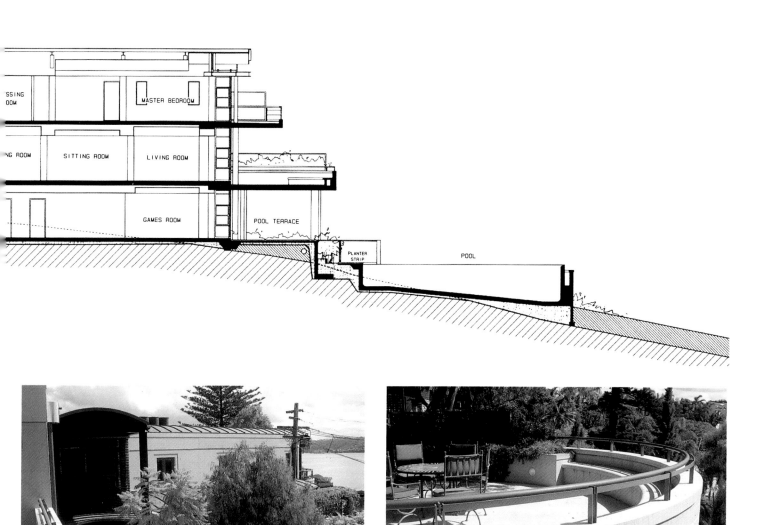

Labels in section drawing:
SSING OOM · MASTER BEDROOM · NG ROOM · SITTING ROOM · LIVING ROOM · GAMES ROOM · POOL TERRACE · PLANTER STRIP · POOL

5

6

7

8

9

10

9   Upper stair and gallery
10 Side gallery
11 Entry level plan
12 Pool terrace level plan
13 Dining and living room opening onto terrace
14 Fireplace inglenook
15 Living room

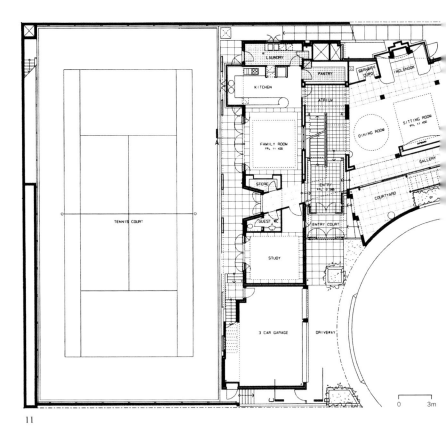

11

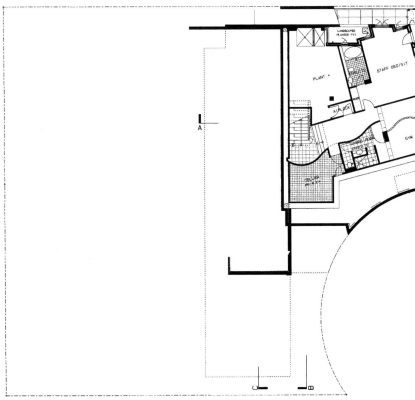

12

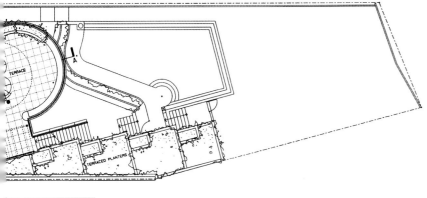

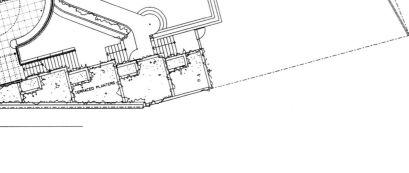

13

14

15

Blood Bank and Laboratories

Design/Completion 1992/1995
Parramatta, New South Wales
Public Works Department, NSW Red Cross
2,000 square metres
Reinforced concrete frame with steel roof
Concrete, face brick, steel, aluminium panels

The Blood Bank presents itself as a kind of social centre, building up a clientele of regular donors and rewarding their contribution with a welcoming and relaxing atmosphere. Location in a central, prominent place and good urban presentation are both important. The building design addresses these public issues. The strong roof form and wide eaves help to establish a presence in Parramatta's most important street where most of the buildings are of a large scale.

The plan is in two sections: a free form space for public access, screening and relaxation areas with a largely glazed administration area above; and a rectangular, more enclosed space in face brickwork which contains the donor room, laboratories, storage and distribution areas.

2

1   George Street entrance at night
2   Entrance from small square
3   Reception areas at night with Federal Law Courts
    in the background
Opposite:
    Reception

1

3

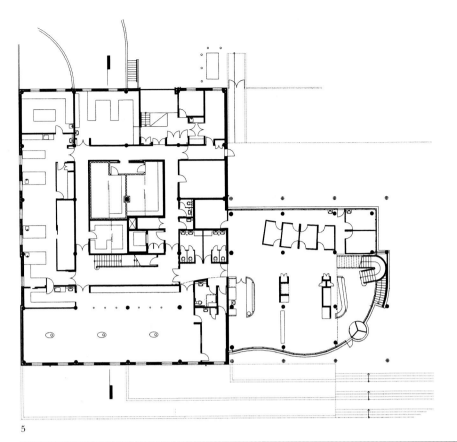

5

6

7

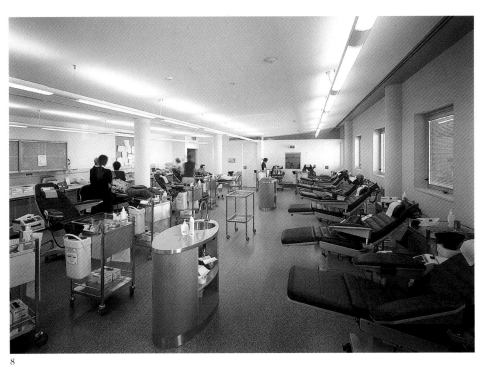

5   Ground floor plan
6   Staff stair hall to laboratory
7   Cafe for donors
8   Donor room
9   Conference room

8

9

Sydney Airport Control Tower

Design/Completion 1992/1994
Botany Bay, New South Wales
Civil Aviation Authority
1,160 square metres
Precast, prefabricated concrete; post-tensioned steel-stayed structure
Stainless steel, aluminium sheeting, glass

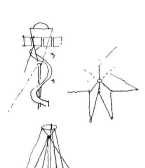

This unique structure was the result of a reassessment of the logic of the conventional control tower. It consists of a top "cabin" with all-round visibility achieved by angled frameless glass. The design has only one central column from which the roof cantilevers, stabilised by stainless steel rods in the glass joints. Above the cabin is the surface movement radar sensor and a corona of aerials and lightning conductors.

Below the cabin is the main deck containing electronic equipment and plant rooms, a duty staff rest area, toilets and a management office. The six pods of the deck are arranged like a cloverleaf. At the base is a circular building with plant room, standby generator, uninterrupted power supply, equipment rooms, staff amenities and management offices. The overall height of the structure is 45 metres.

The geometry of the design is based on an equilateral triangle or tri-star plan with a slim precast central column which contains the services and supports a steel-strutted and cantilevered platform. This is braced by post-tensioned steel rods to three points on the base building, which is itself supported on deep piles. The load of the base building thus serves to stabilise the tower. This ensures the most rigid, sway-free structure with the advantage of prefabrication for rapid construction.

To maintain the visual clarity of this stayed-mast structure, the lift runs on the outside of the central column and the escape stair moves in a large spiral well away from it. The effect is a striking one, demonstrating the advanced technology appropriate to its purpose and its associations with aircraft. All construction is lightweight, prefabricated and weather-protected against the extreme terrain exposure.

1

1   Overall view
2   Plans
3   Control cabin floor plan
4   Support detail
5   Structural detail
6   Entrance court

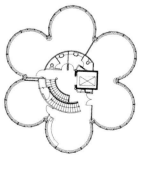
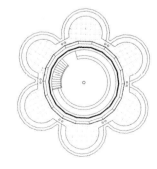

2

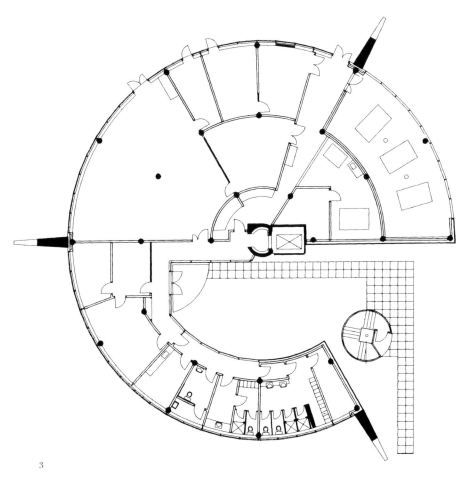

3

4

5

6

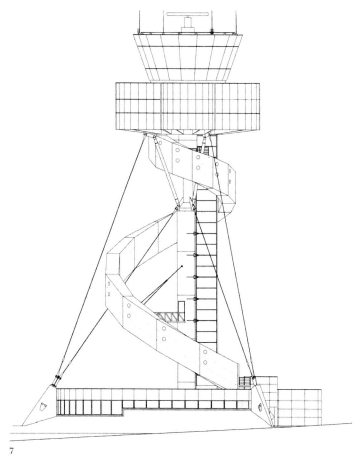

7

7   Elevation
8   Cabin interior
9   Elevation

8

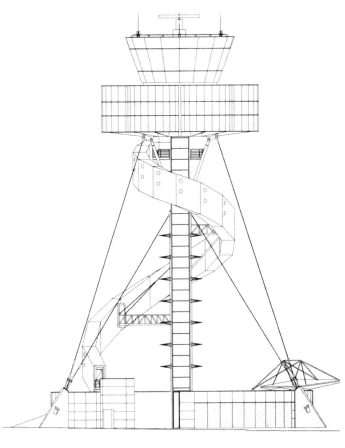

9

Garvan Institute of Medical Research

Design/Completion 1993/1995
Darlinghurst, New South Wales
Garvan Institute of Medical Research
16,500 square metres
Reinforced concrete, steel roof
New aluminium windows in existing brickwork, painted render,
aluminium sandwich panels, steel roofing

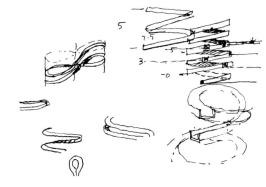

The Garvan Institute of Medical Research was designed for divisions of the Garvan Institute and a number of associated research institutions. The site included a substantial brick and concrete nurses' home surplus to St Vincent's Hospital, which was adapted for reuse as laboratories. Its courtyard was restructured as an atrium with all major circulation taking place around its galleries and spiral stair, which evolved from DNA geometry as a symbol for the institution.

The result meets the institutes' functional needs and is an attractive building both for its users and as a public institution. However, due to its method of project delivery it falls far short of its agreed design and its promise as a civic and architectural entity. It is a useful case study in the value placed on quality and consistency.

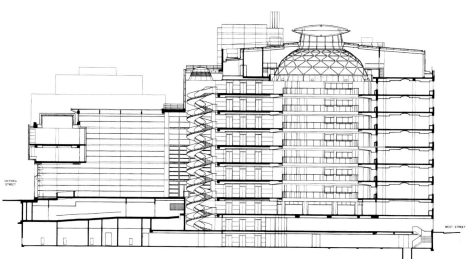

2

1   Old hospital: view down Victoria Street
2   Long section showing entrance gallery, spiral
    stair and atrium
3   New administration section with laboratories
    behind, in the former nurses' home
Opposite:
    Atrium with entrance gallery beyond

1

3

Opposite:
Atrium in former courtyard of the nurses' home
6 Main floor plan
7 Stair from the entrance gallery
8 Spiral stair

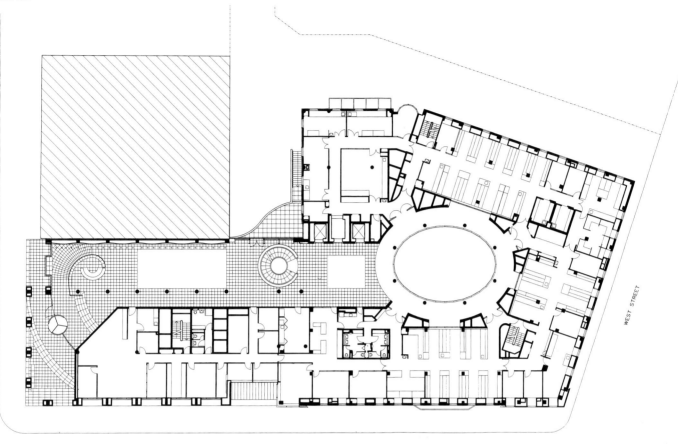

6

7

8

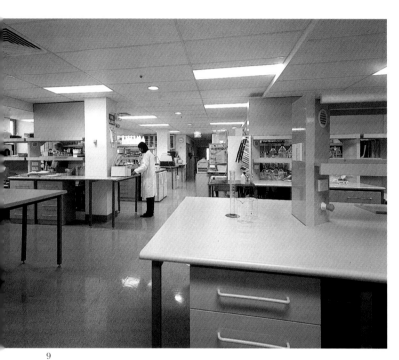

9

10

11

9 Typical research laboratory
10 Theatre for conferences
11 Atrium galleries as circulation between
    laboratory units

Pettit House, Terrey Hills

Design/Completion 1993/1995
Sydney, New South Wales
Brian Pettit
700 square metres
Concrete frame, masonry infill
Rendered and lime-washed brick, stained timber,
steel roofing, marble floors

The site is wedge-shaped, widening out from a narrow street frontage to a broad garden terrace on the edge of a lake, with a view of a golf course on the opposite side. The flat site suggested a multiple courtyard plan, commencing at the street with garages and entry and gradually expanding through guest and service rooms to the main living quarters and long verandah facing north across the lake.

This progression of available width led to the idea of a series of vaulted roofs disposed across the site. Because the use of the rooms demanded larger spaces towards the north, the span of the vaults increases, as does the size of the courtyards. The plan thus becomes a progressive expansion of scale commensurate with the importance of the rooms. As movement through the house is quite extended, the corridor system is staggered as it passes the series of courtyards, introducing vistas of side-lit walls.

1   Courtyard
2   North elevation

1

2

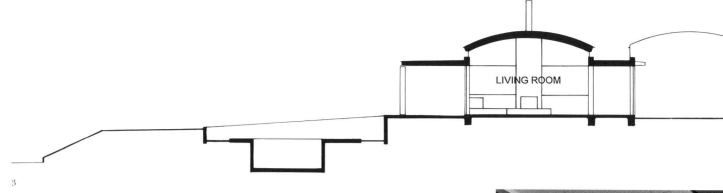

LIVING ROOM

3

3 Section
4 Floor plan
5 Entrance
6 Screened courtyard

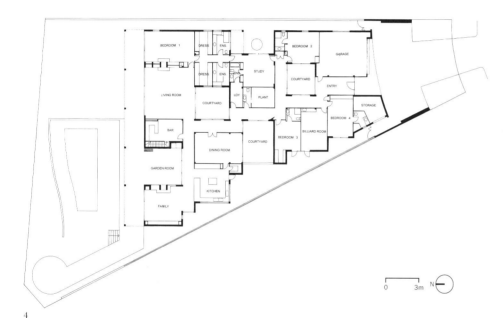

4

0   3m   N

5

6

ENTRY

7

8

9

10

The Education Building

Design/Completion 1994/1996
Sydney, New South Wales
NSW Public Works Department
17,500 square metres over eight levels
Lightweight steel truss structure to new circulation galleries
Glass curtain wall in steel framing

Occupying an entire city block, this project is a landmark sandstone building formed by the old Department of Education Building and the Department of Agriculture, originally built of sandstone in Federation Classical style in two stages. The brief was to retain and restore several heritage areas within the building while modernising existing services and office space.

Previous internal modifications had inserted substantial elements such as lift towers and stair shafts within the light well without solving the problem of circulation between the two isolated cores. This left the traditional centre corridor plan with small offices opening off it. The refurbishment and fitout of the new arrangement was to provide central office accommodation for various administrative sections of the Education Department.

The design inserted new circulation galleries inside the light well courtyard, allowing the access to bypass the office spaces and link the two lift cores and two street entrances. The galleries are lightweight steel and glass structures suspended from the top edge of the light well. Eliminating the central corridors resulted in a substantial increase in usable floor area.

1

2

3

4

1 Sandstone facades to Farrar Place
2 Detail of glazed galleries
3 Suspended corridors in old courtyard
4 Wider access gallery at entrance level
5 Main entrance gallery connection

5

6

7

6 Restored rooftop art gallery
7 Restored meeting room interior
8 Entrance level floor plan showing gallery and
   courtyard
9 Section showing suspended steel galleries in the
   courtyard
10 Restored entrance lobby

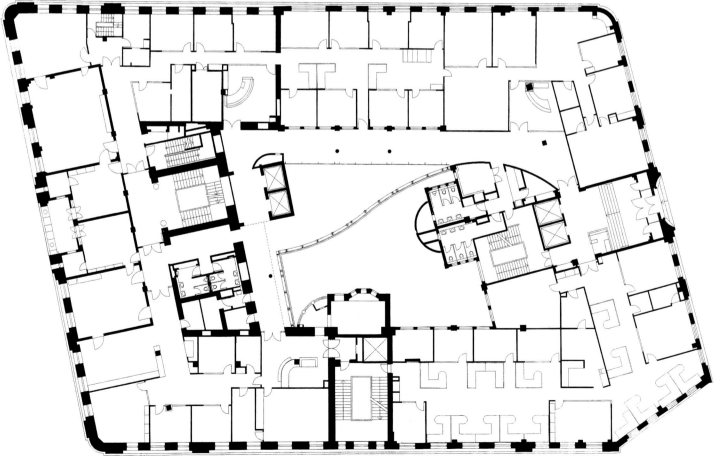

8

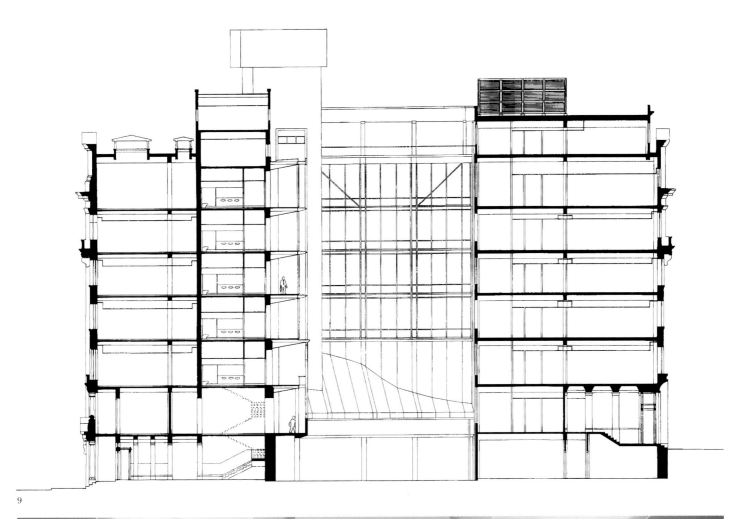

9

10

Royal Agricultural Showground Exhibition Halls and Administration Building

Design/Completion 1996/1998
Homebush Bay, New South Wales
Olympic Co-ordination Authority
34,000 square metres
Long-span domed and vaulted structures, post-tensioned and conventional reinforced concrete structures, reinforced concrete ring beam and columns
Reinforced concrete, laminated plantation timber, unpainted galvanised steel, face brickwork, glazed tile, lightweight metal panels, roll-formed steel roof sheeting, teflon/fibreglass awnings

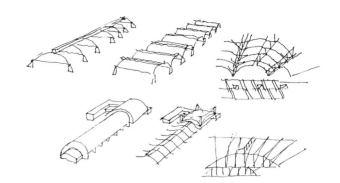

The permanent use of the new building is as the main exhibition halls of the Sydney Showgrounds, but an overriding factor in the design was their scheduled use for indoor sports at the Sydney Olympics in 2000. Span and height were determined by the requirement for 25,000 seats and four indoor competition spaces, with the largest under the dome to seat 10,000. The continuous 325-metre-long space is naturally ventilated and can be opened up along the sides to public outdoor spaces and for servicing. Natural lighting in general use can be controlled for exhibitions. During the Royal Easter Show as many as 200,000 people per day pass through these spaces.

Government policy for ecologically sustainable development encouraged natural ventilation and the use of laminated plantation timber for the primary structure, incorporating dome and vault forms with highly stressed steel jointing and tension members. The 100-metre-diameter dome forms part of the Royal Agricultural Show administration building, which serves as an entrance portal to the enclosed showground. The corner tower will carry electronic communication elements and signs.

1 Aerial view during the Easter Show
2 Longitudinal section
3 Entrance canopy
4 Administration building and main entrance

1

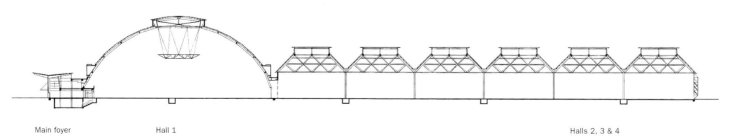

Main foyer   Hall 1   Halls 2, 3 & 4

2

3

4

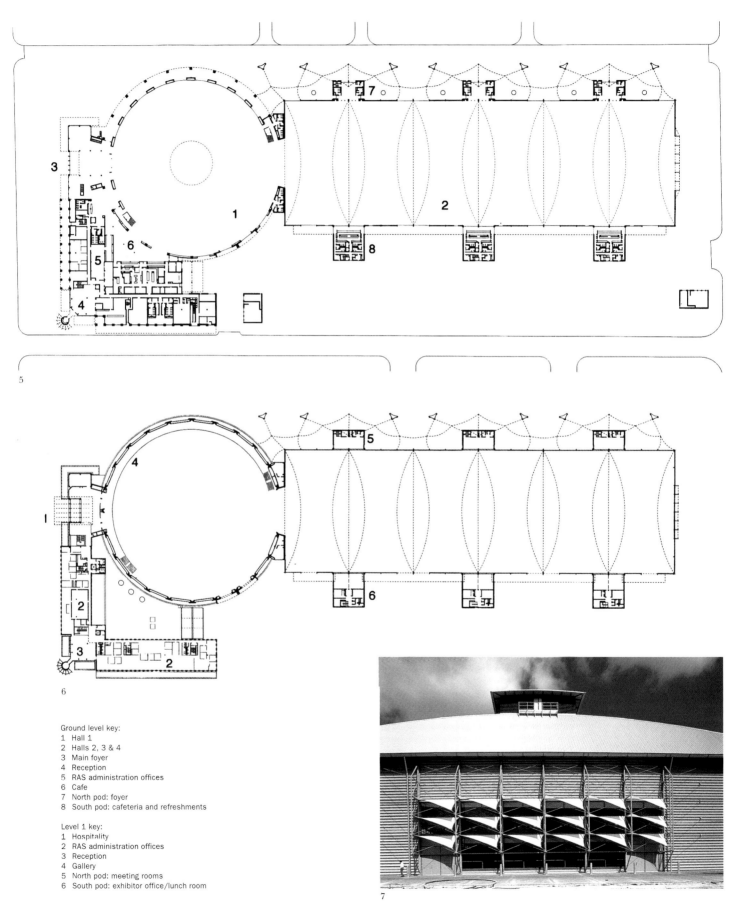

5

6

Ground level key:
1 Hall 1
2 Halls 2, 3 & 4
3 Main foyer
4 Reception
5 RAS administration offices
6 Cafe
7 North pod: foyer
8 South pod: cafeteria and refreshments

Level 1 key:
1 Hospitality
2 RAS administration offices
3 Reception
4 Gallery
5 North pod: meeting rooms
6 South pod: exhibitor office/lunch room

7

5　Ground level floor plan
6　Level 1 floor plan
7　East elevation detail
8　Teflon/fibreglass awning as public shelter on the north side
9　Fabric awning
10　The dome
Following pages:
　　Dome interior with exhibition in progress

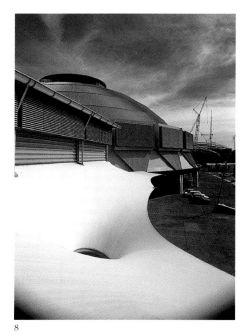

8

9

10

12 Bay windows of the dome
13 Entrance hall and canopy
14 Exhibition halls

12

13

14

State Hockey Centre

Design/Completion 1997/1998
Homebush Bay, New South Wales
Olympic Co-ordination Authority
4,370 square metres
Suspended steel roof, reinforced concrete grandstand
Face brickwork, off-form concrete, steel primary and secondary structures
(painted), perforated steel screens

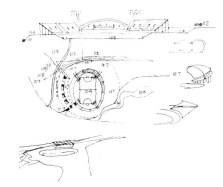

The State Hockey Centre is a new facility for 5,000 spectators with the capacity to expand to seat 15,000 for the Sydney Olympics. Player, administration and spectator facilities are accommodated on three levels under the grandstand on the western side of the new hockey pitch.

The sloping site, existing car parks and sports centre, and the adjoining creek provided some constraints. Also important were the geometry of the spectator sight-lines and pitch orientation, and the need to address entry from the west in permanent mode and entry from Olympic Boulevard on the other side during the Olympic Games.

The grandstand structure rests on the concourse and creates the entry focal point and interface between the forecourt and pitch, while the player change rooms are below, at the level of the pitch. The concourse forms a large, flat, elliptical terrace taking up the slope of the site, with the pitch recessed into it like a bowl. The flat terrace allows easy assembly of temporary seating and facilitates crowd management.

The lighting towers are unusual, adapting the idea of an angled desk lamp to put the lights at the ideal place and angle. The masts are skewed both in plan and elevation, taking them out of the sight-lines of the temporary Olympic Games seating.

The form of the grandstand was generated from sight-line studies and the requirements of the brief to provide separate grandstand and arena seating as well as ensuring a view of the entire pitch from inside the VIP function room. The dramatic roof form is independent of the grandstand structure, being hung from a mast at the rear and tied down by inverted catenaries which are brought down at the two ends. Consequently, the seating geometry is free of the roof and of stresses arising from roof movement, and the roof itself is able to be extremely light.

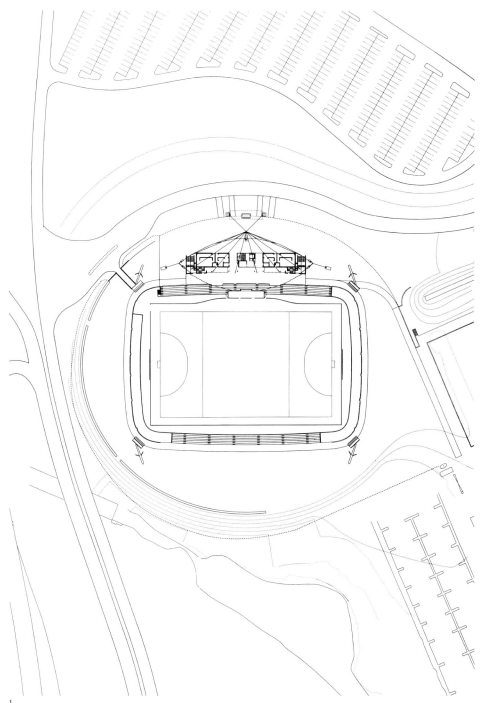

1

1 Site plan
2 Section
3 Angled masts set lights in optimum position

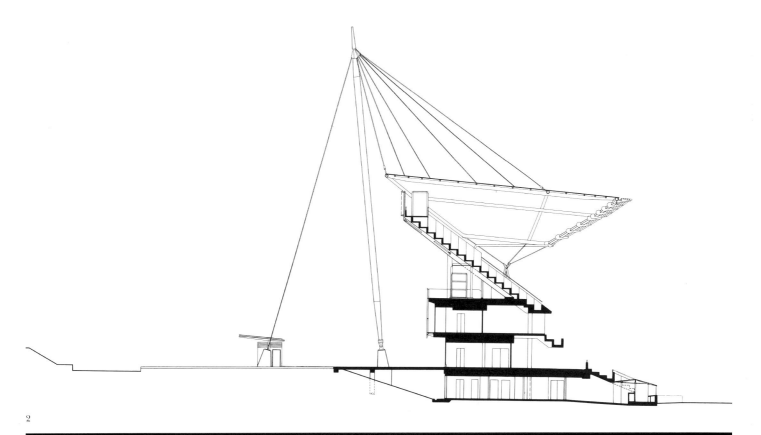

2

3

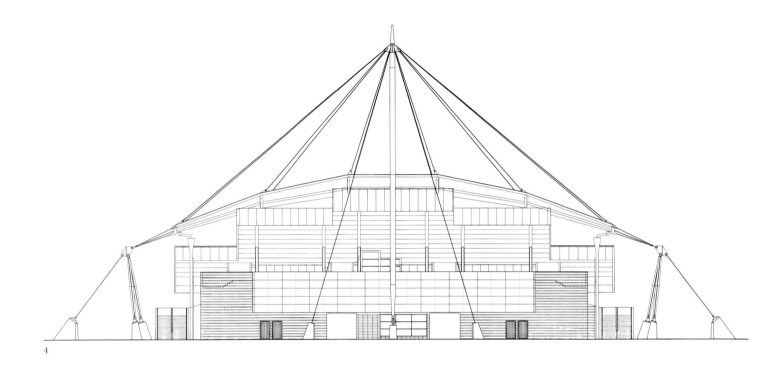

4

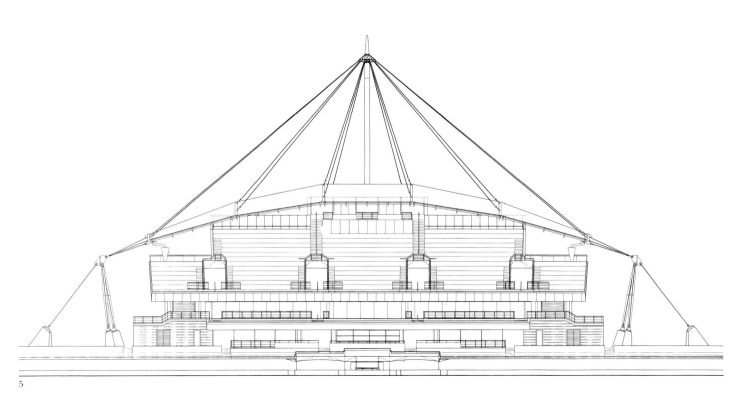

5

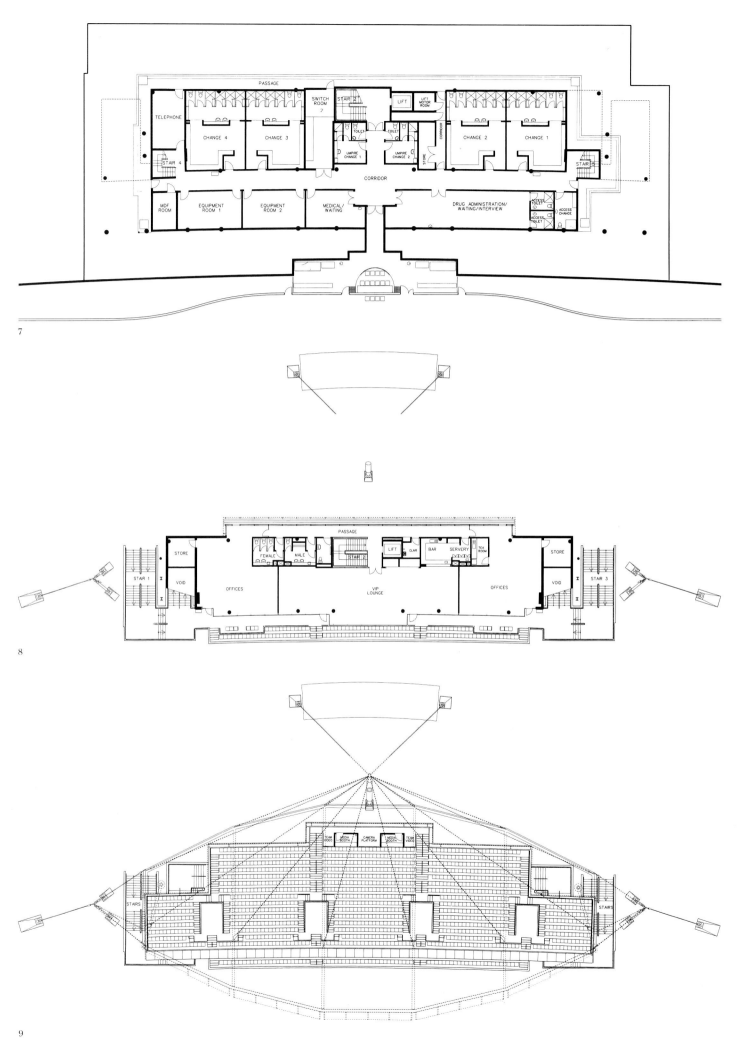

7

8

9

7　Changing rooms at pitch level
8　Administration and VIP viewing lounge
9　Public seating tiers
10　Roof suspended from a single mast; backstays form the gate posts
11　Pitch set down in an oval terrace
Following pages:
　　View of the pitch from the back of the grandstand

10

11

Sydney Convention Centre

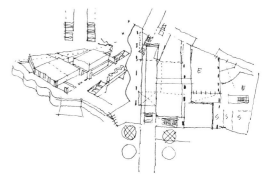

Design/Completion 1997/1999
Darling Harbour, Sydney, New South Wales
Darling Harbour Authority
19,000 square metres
Reinforced concrete and steel on deep piles
Off-form concrete, glass block, steel, zinc sheeting, veneer plywood, plasterboard, carpet, bluestone, sandstone

This building links the original large conference centre and the exhibition centre, two important buildings designed by other architects. It completes the arrangement and provides central registration and management together with a 1,000-seat auditorium, a 1,000-seat banquet hall and 2,200 square metres of conjoined exhibition space, plus a variety of conference rooms. The site lies beneath a complex of freeways whose columns penetrate but cannot be utilised. Earlier concepts could not be realised due to height limitations imposed by the roadways, which rise, tilt and interweave above the conference centre.

A new elevated entrance for taxis and coaches is achieved on the west, linked to the east waterfront entrance and intersecting the original north–south linkage of the conference centre and exhibition halls. Where the new building asserts itself and faces the waterfront, the huge freeway structures are so dominant that the design is refined into large gestures—a frameless, sloping and angled glass facade cantilevered 10 metres out from the main structure, avoiding the use of small-scale building columns. The freeway columns are encompassed within stone-clad walls, penetrated by portals, so that awareness of their presence is suppressed.

1 Montage showing convention centre with exhibition halls to the left, conference hall and casino to the right
2 Pedestrian entrance at Darling Harbour side
3 Stainless steel structure for glazing
4 Space under the freeways for the auditoriums

1

2

3

4

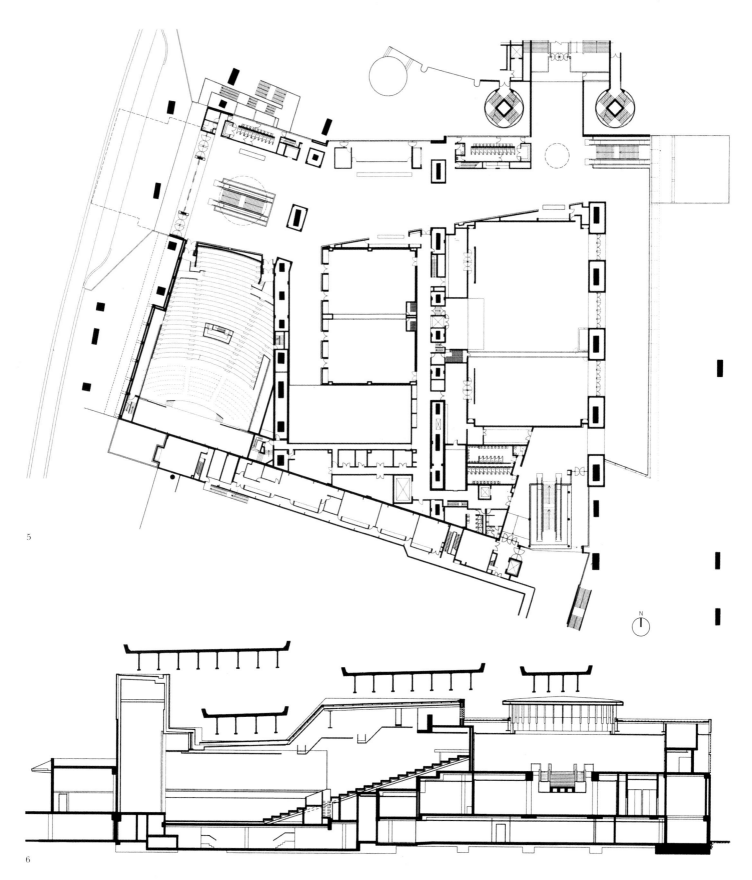

5

6

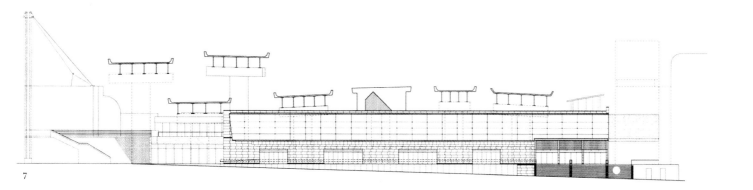

7

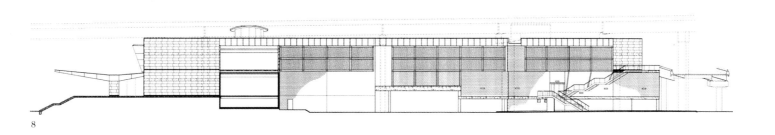

8

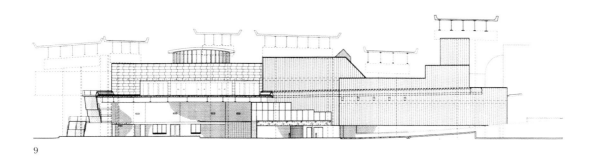

9

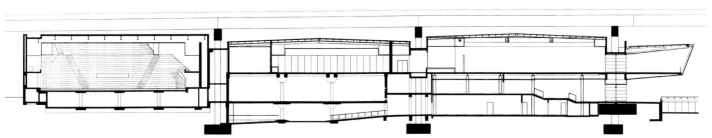

10

11

12

13

July 03 Istanbul

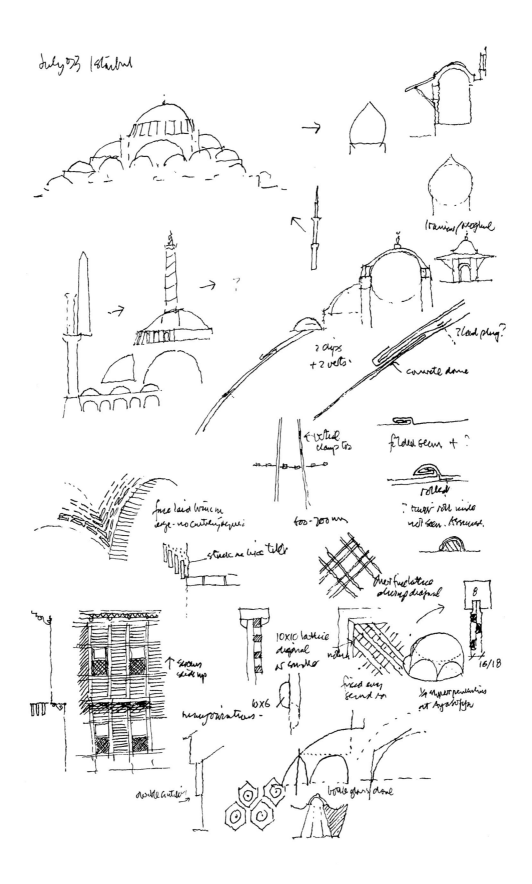

Firm Profile

Biographies

Ken Woolley, AM, BArch, LFRAIA
Chairman & Design Director, Ancher Mortlock & Woolley

Ken Woolley was born in Sydney in 1933 and studied architecture at the University of Sydney, where he graduated with first class honours and the University Medal in 1955. With Peter Webber he was a founding member of the special design team in Harry Rembert's Design Office of the NSW Government Architect's Branch, and soon became involved in major projects such as Fisher Library and the State Office Block.

His own house at Mosman (1962) won the Wilkinson Award and paved the way for private practice, with a commission for project housing for Pettit & Sevitt. He joined the partnership Ancher Mortlock Murray & Woolley in 1964, just prior to Sydney Ancher's retirement. This practice (which became Ancher Mortlock & Woolley in 1976) has received all the major Australian architectural awards and has created numerous outstanding buildings, including the Australian Embassy, Bangkok; Town Hall House, Sydney; the Park Hyatt, Campbells Cove; the ABC Centre, Ultimo; the Victorian State Library, Melbourne; the Control Tower at Sydney Airport; the RAS Exhibition Halls/Olympics Indoor Sports Stadium and the State Hockey Centre, Homebush Bay; and the Sydney Convention Centre, Darling Harbour.

Ken Woolley has been a visiting professor at the University of Sydney and the University of NSW, and has served as chairman or member of numerous awards, review and competition juries. He was made a Member of the Order of Australia in 1988 and was awarded the Gold Medal of the Royal Australian Institute of Architects in 1993.

Steve Thomas BArch, FRAIA
Director, Ancher Mortlock & Woolley

Steve Thomas was born in Newcastle in 1941. He studied at the University of NSW Newcastle College of Architecture where he received his Bachelor of Architecture degree and was awarded the inaugural James Hardie Award for Architectural Design.

He joined Ancher Mortlock & Woolley in 1969 and has been a director since 1974. He travelled and studied in the USA and Europe in 1977, 1982, 1984 and 1988.

In the roles of Project Director or Design Manager, Steve has been involved in the master planning, design and documentation, and management of major projects for the practice, including residential, academic and public buildings. Among these are Linley Cove medium density housing; Yarralumla Shores, Canberra; and the Newcastle University Great Hall and Stages 3 and 4 of the Student Union. He was also involved in the GMLS and West Wharf Amenities on Garden Island, the ADF Cadets Mess in Canberra, and the Sydney Airport Control Tower.

He was a member of the design team for the successful competitions for the National Archives (1983) and the Victorian State Library and Museum (1985). His recent work includes acting as Project Director for the ABC Radio and Orchestra Building; the RAS Exhibition Halls, Homebush Bay; and the Sydney Convention Centre South, Darling Harbour—all major projects requiring the management of multidisciplinary teams on buildings with highly complex structural services and functional requirements.

Dale Swan BArch (Hons), MSc, FRAIA
Director, Ancher Mortlock & Woolley

Dale Swan was born in Sydney in 1948 and studied architecture at what is now the University of Technology, Sydney, graduating with first class honours in 1971. He completed a Master of Science in Environmental Studies at Heriot Watt University, Edinburgh, in 1974. Between 1971 and 1974 he worked and studied in the UK and travelled in Europe and the USA.

He has studied a number of building types overseas, and for special projects has been to Japan, South East Asia, Canada and most recently to Atlanta, USA, to inspect the Olympic facilities.

Dale has been a director of Ancher Mortlock & Woolley since 1982. He is involved in all aspects of the practice, including master planning, brief development, feasibility studies, concept design and design development, and has acquired specialised knowledge of research laboratory buildings and hotels.

Important projects in which he has been involved include the Mormon Chapel at Leura; the Arc Glasshouses, Sydney Botanic Gardens; the Australian Pavilion at Expo 88; the Children's Medical Research Institute; the Garvan Institute of Medical Research; the Blood Bank and Laboratories, Parramatta; the Education Building, Sydney; the Walsh Bay Redevelopment; the State Hockey Centre, Homebush Bay; Hill Road Amenities, Homebush Bay; Sand River Golf and Sports Club in Shenzhen, China; and numerous domestic and international competitions.

He has lectured at the University of NSW and University of Technology and served on design juries. He is currently involved with the RAIA NSW Chapter Bulletin Editorial Committee and Practice Committee and the Board of Architects' Committee of Review.

Philip Baigent BSc (Arch), BArch (Hons), ARAIA
Director, Ancher Mortlock & Woolley

Philip Baigent was born in Sydney in 1955. He studied at the University of NSW and graduated with first class honours in 1980. He was awarded the James Hardie Award for academic achievement during his Bachelor of Architecture degree.

After the completion of his university studies, Philip worked in the office of Michael Hesse and Associates, joining Ancher Mortlock & Woolley in 1981. Following an intensive study tour of Europe, Egypt and Scandinavia, he rejoined the office of Ancher Mortlock & Woolley and became an Associate in 1986. In 1993 he travelled in Europe on a lighting study grant. He became a Director of the practice in 1993.

With 15 years in the profession, Philip has acquired experience in all aspects of architectural practice, from master planning and concept design through to the management of documentation teams, including fast track documentation delivery systems and contract administration roles. Over the past five years, he has been responsible for the documentation and implementation of the office's QA system and until recently was Quality Manager.

He has had extensive experience with many residential, academic, and major public and government building projects. He has been the Project Architect for the Australian Pavilion at Expo 88 and the ABC Radio and Orchestra Centre at Ultimo. Most recently he has worked as the Assistant Project Director for the RAS Exhibition Halls at Homebush Bay and as Project Director for the State Library of Victoria redevelopment project in Melbourne. This project has been constructed to date in five stages over a nine-year period and involves new extensions, infills, refurbishment and heritage restoration works.

Philip has gained experience in developing strategies to address various architectural issues. These include construction works staging and furniture decant relocations; participation in ESD forums; office competition submissions; and involvement in the development of client briefs for the State Library of Victoria project and the Homebush Bay Multi-Use Arena for the Olympic Co-ordination Authority.

Lynn Vlismas BArch (Hons), ARAIA
Associate, Ancher Mortlock & Woolley

Lynn Vlismas was born in Murwillumbah, NSW, in 1950. In 1968 she moved to Sydney to study architecture at the University of NSW where she graduated with honours in 1974. During 1975 she worked with Hely and Horne until undertaking a study tour of South East Asia and China, after which she was employed by Civil and Civic to work on interior fitout projects. Awarded a working scholarship, Lynn went to Norway during the latter half of 1977, which also provided an opportunity to study the work of Alvar Aalto in Finland.

Since joining Ancher Mortlock & Woolley in 1980 she has been involved in many of the firm's major projects, including Australian Pavilion, Expo 88, Brisbane; Commonwealth Law Courts, Parramatta; Yarralumla Shores, Canberra; ABC Radio and Orchestra Centre, Ultimo; Children's Medical Research Institute, Westmead; Blood Bank and Laboratories, Parramatta; Garvan Institute of Medical Research, Darlinghurst; the refurbishment and fitout of the Education Building, Sydney; and the Sydney City Council office lobby and exhibition area fitout at Town Hall House, Sydney. She has also been involved at a senior level in the RAS Exhibition Halls and Administration Building, Homebush Bay, and the new courtyard reading rooms and the historically significant dome reading room refurbishment at the State Library of Victoria, Melbourne.

Lynn became an Associate of Ancher Mortlock & Woolley in 1988. Her professional interests have involved her with the RAIA Bulletin Committee and university design groups, and she has served as a university design juror.

Garry Wallace BSc (Arch), BArch (Hons), ARAIA
Associate, Ancher Mortlock & Woolley

Garry Wallace was born in Leeton, NSW, in 1954. He studied architecture at the University of NSW, Sydney, and graduated in 1985 with first class honours. He travelled and studied in Europe and Japan in 1977 and 1982.

Garry has worked at a senior level for a number of Sydney-based architectural practices, including Devine Erby Mazlin. He has been involved in the Australian Defence Force Academy Cadets Mess, Canberra; Commonwealth Law Courts, Parramatta; Garvan Institute of Medical Research, Darlinghurst; the Education Building refurbishment, Sydney; and the RAS Exhibition Halls, Homebush Bay.

His experience on a wide range of architectural projects includes large and complex institutional buildings, large commercial fitouts, and medium- and high-rise residential buildings. He has a background in environmental design issues and the research, design and construction of solar housing. He has been involved with the Royal Australian Institute of Architects (NSW Chapter) ESD Committee in the publication of the National Environment Policy and Environment Design Guides, and has been a university tutor in architectural science subjects.

Robin Yeap BSc (Arch), BArch, MSc (Arch), ARAIA
Associate, Ancher Mortlock & Woolley

Robin Yeap was born in Singapore in 1957 and studied architecture at Sydney University, graduating in 1983. In 1988 he undertook the Masters Degree in Building Design at Columbia University in New York. Remaining in New York, he worked with I.M. Pei and Partners on conference and trade centres in Washington and Barcelona until 1992. In Sydney he has worked with Philip Cox & Partners and Bruce Eeles & Associates, being involved in Darling Harbour projects, hospitals and colleges.

Robin became an Associate with Ancher Mortlock & Woolley in 1994 and has been involved in such major projects as ABC Radio and Orchestra Centre, Ultimo; Australian Pavilion at Expo 88, Brisbane; Park Hyatt Hotel, Campbells Cove; Walsh Bay Redevelopment, Sydney; Royal Botanic Gardens Visitor's Centre, Sydney; Garvan Institute of Medical Research, Darlinghurst; Victorian State Library Directorate Building and public spaces, Melbourne; RAS Exhibition Halls and the State Hockey Centre at Homebush Bay; and various apartment buildings.

He has served as visiting design critic at the Pratt Institute at Sydney University and at the University of NSW, and has special interest in the fields of public space and building design.

Arthur Chapman BSc (Arch), BArch, MBA, RAIA, MAICD, AIMM, JP
Practice Manager, Ancher Mortlock & Woolley

Arthur Chapman was born in Quirindi, NSW, in 1962. He received a Bachelor of Science in Architecture degree from the University of Newcastle in 1987 and a Bachelor of Architecture degree from the University of New South Wales in 1991. At the Macquarie University Graduate School of Management, he received a Master of Business Administration degree in 1998.

Arthur began his architectural experience in the one-man practice of Victor Dellit, dealing with all facets of architecture. He then spent several years as a contract architect working on a range of projects for practices including Davenport Campbell and Devine Erby Mazlin. Developing a career in management, he worked for several years in sales and distribution management before joining Ancher Mortlock & Woolley as Practice Manager in 1996.

As Practice Manager, Arthur is responsible for the management of all the firm's operations in many projects of significance, including the RAS Exhibition Halls and State Hockey Centre at Homebush Bay and the Sydney Convention Centre at Darling Harbour. His activities include submissions of consultant selection, preparation of client and sub-consultant contracts, engagement of staff and suppliers, and management responsibility for IT and accounting services, premises, resource programming and financial controls.

Chronological List of Buildings and Projects

1955

Chapel and Sisters' Home, St Margaret's Hospital
Sydney, NSW
Government Architect's Office
Completed 1958

Chemistry School, University of Sydney
Sydney, NSW
Completed 1959
With H. Rembert and P. Webber,
Government Architect's Office

1958

**Low Cost Exhibition House
Taubman's Family House**
Cherrybrooke, Pennant Hills, NSW
National competition winner
With Michael Dysart
Constructed 1959

Fisher Library, University of Sydney
Camperdown, NSW
Joint architects: NSW Government
Architect and T.E. O'Mahony
Design architect: Ken Woolley

Millar House
Shell Cove Road, Cronulla, NSW

1959

Descon Factory
Brookvale, NSW
(Now demolished)

1960

Mona Vale Hospital
Mona Vale, NSW
With C. Weatherburn, Government
Architect's Office
(Has since been extensively altered)

Recreation Hall and Chapel
Lidcombe State Hospital, NSW
Government Architect's Office
Completed 1962

State Office Block
Macquarie, Bent and Philip Streets,
Sydney, NSW
Government Architect's Office
Completed 1965, demolished 1998

Schatz House
25 Church Street, Pymble, NSW

1961

Woolley House, Mosman
34 Bullecourt Avenue, Mosman, NSW
Completed 1962

Three Exhibition Houses
Kingsdene, NSW
Lend Lease Homes
Completed 1962
With Michael Dysart

Windsor Courthouse (1819)
Francis Greenway, Windsor, NSW
Restoration
Government Architect's Office

Early Project House Designs
Pettit & Sevitt

1962

Macquarie Field House (1843) Restoration
Near Liverpool, NSW
David Jamieson and Department of Lands

1963

Spiral Fountain, State Office Block
Bent Street, Sydney, NSW
Completed 1965
(Now demolished)

Baudish House
40 Greenfield Avenue, Middle Cove, NSW
Completed 1963

1964

Pettit & Sevitt Houses
Richmond Avenue, St Ives, NSW
(Demonstration village)
3,500 houses eventually built

Culhane House
George Street, Hunters Hill, NSW

Rothery House
Strathfield, NSW
(Since destroyed by fire)

Theatrette and Premier's Suite Interiors
State Office Block, Bent Street, Sydney,
NSW
Private commission

**University of Newcastle Student Union,
Stage 1**
Newcastle, NSW
Completed 1967

F.C. Pye Field Environment Laboratory
Black Mountain, Canberra, ACT
CSIRO
Completed 1966

1965

Myers House
Carrington Road, Mosman, NSW
(Since demolished)

The Penthouses
Darling Point, NSW
Completed 1968

**Macquarie University Student Union
Building, Stage 1**
North Ryde, NSW
Completed 1969; later stages and
alterations by other architects; now
unrecognisable
With Bryce Mortlock

RAIA Headquarters Building
Mugga Way, Canberra
Royal Australian Institute of Architects
Bryce Mortlock, Ken Woolley and Stuart
Murray collaboration following
unsuccessful Ancher proposal

1966

ULLR Ski Lodge
Perisher Valley, NSW

The Cottages
116 Milson Road, Cremorne Point, NSW
Six townhouses

Hann House
Stuart Street, Blakehurst, NSW

1967

Macquarie Town Housing
Ryde, NSW
400 dwellings (unbuilt)

Six Townhouses
Gillies Street, Wollstonecraft, NSW
Span Developments
Completed 1968

Wollstonecraft Flats
66–68 Shirley Road, Wollstonecraft,
Sydney, NSW
Strata Developments
30 flats on two L-shaped blocks

Five Townhouses
18 Shirley Road, Wollstonecraft,
Sydney, NSW
Span Developments

**University of Newcastle Student Union
Building, Stage 2/Staff House,
University of Newcastle**
Newcastle, NSW
Completed 1974

Seventh Day Adventist Church
Turner, Canberra, ACT
Completed 1971

Fernhurst Avenue, Cremorne
Cremorne, Sydney, NSW
Nine townhouses for Strata Development
Stuart Murray

"Deepdene"
Elizabeth Bay Road, Sydney, NSW
Seven-storey complex of five apartments
Stuart Murray

1968

National Gallery Competition
Canberra, ACT
Highly commended (effectively second
prize)

Kindergarten
La Perouse, NSW
Based on a Pettit & Sevitt house

Six-Storey Apartments
Fairfax Road, Bellevue Hill, NSW

Noble Lowndes Hotel and Apartments
Kings Cross, Sydney, NSW
(Unbuilt)

**Wentworth Student Union Building,
Stage 1**
University of Sydney, NSW
Completed 1971

Mosman Townhouses
20–22 Almora Street, Mosman,
Sydney, NSW
Span Investments
Completed 1972
Bryce Mortlock

1969

BHP Steel House for the Future
Research project and report

Small Office Building
16 Atchison Street, St Leonards, NSW

12-Storey Apartment Building
Reynolds Street, Cremorne, NSW
Completed 1972

Three Project Houses
Perth, WA
Corser Homes

**University of Newcastle Student Union,
Stage 3**
Newcastle, NSW
Completed 1971

Housing Research Project
Canberra, ACT
"Suburban Experiment" report for NCDC

1970

**Town Hall House, Sydney Square and
Town Hall Refurbishment**
Sydney, NSW
New office building and Town Hall House
completed 1974; other work completed
1977

Government Detached and Atrium Houses
Canberra, ACT
600 houses
Completed 1978

St Andrew's Cathedral Restoration
Sydney, NSW
National Trust grant

**Woden Churches Centre and Office
Building**
Phillip Town Centre, Canberra, ACT

**Woden OA School for Intellectually
Handicapped Children**
Canberra, ACT

1972

Victoria Point Apartments
Victoria Street, Potts Point, Sydney, NSW
500 units (unbuilt)

Phillip Health Centre
Phillip, Canberra, ACT
Completed 1975

Woden District Library
Phillip, Canberra, ACT
Completed 1977

1973

Woden Child Care Centre
Canberra, ACT
Completed 1978

Macquarie Fields Attached Housing
Macquarie Fields, NSW
Housing Commission of NSW

Kippax Health Centre
Moore and Alinga Streets, Canberra, ACT

Pacific Harbour
Fiji
Pettit & Sevitt
100 holiday resort houses

Master Plan for the Commonwealth Scientific and Industrial Research Organisation
Black Mountain Campus, Canberra, ACT
Completed 1975

Australian Embassy, Bangkok
Bangkok, Thailand
Completed 1978

1974

High-Density Housing
Rhodes, Sydney, NSW
(Unbuilt)

Woolloomooloo Action Plan Urban Design Study for the "Three Governments"
Woolloomooloo, Sydney, NSW
Generator of the Woolloomooloo Housing Project

Soi Attakarn Prasit Embassy Housing
Bangkok, Thailand
Australian Government
(Unbuilt)

100 Townhouses and Village Centre
Holsworthy, NSW
New town pilot project (unbuilt)

1975

Pettit House, Garran
Brereton Street, Garran, Canberra, ACT

Precast Concrete House
Research project for Hume Concrete
(unbuilt)

Master Plan and Site Development
Canberra, ACT
Academy of Science

Infill Housing and Victorian Period Houses Restoration
Glebe, NSW
Restoration phase only completed 1978

1976

Rare Book Library, University of Sydney
Sydney, NSW
(Unbuilt)

1,000 Apartments and Urban Development
Darlinghurst Hill, Sydney, NSW
(Unbuilt)

1977

Honiara Radio Station
Honiara, Solomon Islands
Australian Aid Program
Completed 1981

Vila Radio Station
Vila, Vanuatu
Australian Aid Program
Completed 1980

1978

West Amenities Refit and Control Building
Garden Island Naval Dockyard, Sydney, NSW
Completed 1980

Botanic Gardens Kiosk
Sydney, NSW
With NSW Government Architect

Australian Institute of Criminology
Canberra, ACT
Competition winner (unbuilt)

Housing Commission Development, Woolloomooloo
Woolloomooloo, Sydney, NSW
56 houses
Stage 1 (16 houses) completed 1980

Pettit House, Collaroy
Beach Road, Collaroy, NSW

1979

National Archive Headquarters
Canberra, ACT
Competition winner

Central Area Lighting Masterplan Study
Canberra, ACT

1980

The Completion of Engehurst Exhibition
Design concept for RAIA Conference

Linley Cove Housing Development
Lane Cove, NSW
In collaboration with Steve Thomas
220 dwelling units
Stages 1–4 completed 1982–85

Guided Missile Launching System Assembly and Overhaul Building
Garden Island Naval Dockyard, Sydney, NSW
Construction 1982–83

Mormon Chapel
Railway Parade, Leura, NSW
Completed 1983

Woolley House, Paddington
8A Cooper Street, Paddington, NSW

1981

Yarralumla Shores
Black Street, Yarralumla, Canberra, ACT
In collaboration with Steve Thomas
Medium-density lakeside housing
(26 townhouses)
Completed 1983

1982

**Australian Defence Forces Academy
Cadets Mess**
Campbell, ACT
Joint architect with Department
of Housing and Construction

Denning Offices
Pacific Highway, Gordon, NSW
Small office building
Completed 1984

The Anchorage
Tweed Heads, NSW
Lend Lease Corporation
350-unit waterfront housing concept
and master plan; Stage 1 only completed
(22 houses and units)

Pair of houses
Dune Street, Fingal Bay, Tweed Heads,
NSW

Queenscliff Surf Pavilion
Manly, NSW
Manly Council and Pettit/Whiteholme
Completed 1983

Australian Federal Police Headquarters
London Circuit, Civic, Canberra, ACT
Design and documentation (unbuilt)

1983

The Quay Gateway
Circular Quay, Sydney, NSW
RAIA ideas competition winner

Parliamentary Triangle Study
Canberra, ACT
With National Capital Development
Commission

Fleet Wharf
Cowper's Wharf Road
Garden Island, Sydney, NSW

Beauchamp House
Marcus Clark Street, Canberra, ACT
Heritage hostel building converted
to offices for Academy of Science;
renovations and restoration

1984

National Archive Headquarters
Canberra, ACT
Design development stage (unbuilt)

55–57 New Beach Road
Darling Point, NSW
Overlapping apartments

Pettit Weekender
Scotland Island, NSW

Mixed Development
North Steyne, Manly, NSW
Pettit/Whiteholme
Apartments, office, retail

Offices, 93 George Street
Parramatta, NSW
NSW State Superannuation Board and
Pettit/Whiteholme

Woolley House, Palm Beach
21 Florida Road, Palm Beach, NSW
Completed 1986

Portal Building Designs, Naval Dockyard
Garden Island, Sydney, NSW

Commonwealth Law Courts
Parramatta, Sydney, NSW
Completed 1987

Prefabricated Holiday House
NSW south coast
John Queneau Homes

1985

State Library of Victoria
Melbourne, Vic.
Design competition winner (project
scope changed since competition)
Expected completion 2003

**National Archives and Exposition
Design Development**
Central area, Canberra, ACT

"The Arc" Glasshouses
(associated with the pyramid glasshouse)
Royal Botanic Gardens, Sydney, NSW
Completed 1987

1 Macquarie Street
Circular Quay, NSW
Hotel (unbuilt)

Space Theatre, Powerhouse Museum
Sydney, NSW
Omnimax theatre (unbuilt)

Park Hyatt Hotel
Campbells Cove, NSW
Competition winner; development
tender submission
Completed 1989

Pettit Apartments
Manly Beach Plaza
North Steyne, Manly, NSW
Additions and alterations

Elsie Street Office Building
Burwood, NSW
Pettit/Whiteholme

TAFE College Library
Wollongong, NSW
Wollongong TAFE

**Wentworth Student Union Building,
Stage 2**
University of Sydney, NSW

HMAS Penguin
Sydney, NSW
Naval building

St Andrew's Cathedral
George Street, Sydney, NSW
New narthex/east doorway

1986

Australia Pavilion, Expo 88
Brisbane, Qld
Impermanent building for Expo
exhibition
Completed 1988, removed 1989

Park Hyatt Hotel
Campbells Cove, NSW
Completed 1990

The Australian Hellenic War Memorial
Anzac Parade, Canberra, ACT
Winner of a limited competition for
architects and sculptors
Completed 1986

Drug and Alcohol Rehabilitation Centre
155 Keverstone Circuit, Isabella Plains,
Canberra, ACT

ITF Seafarers Centre
Wentworth Avenue, Mascot, NSW
Renovations to bowling club

Wingecarribee Street Mall
Bowral, NSW

1987

Walsh Bay
Sydney, NSW
Competition
Development tender; successful
submission for CRI

HMAS Penguin
Balmoral, Sydney, NSW
Officers' quarters

Health Centre
Tuggeranong, ACT

7 Gladswood Gardens
Double Bay, NSW
6 apartments

Liverpool Town Centre
Corner George and Moore Streets,
Liverpool, NSW
Pettit/Whiteholme
Office building

ABC Radio and Orchestra Centre
Harris Street, Ultimo, Sydney, NSW
Completed 1991

1988

Children's Medical Research Institute
Westmead, Sydney, NSW

Pettit House
Lane-Poole Place, Yarralumla, ACT
Duplex houses

Darling Harbour, East Esplanade
Competition winner
Development tender submission

1989

State Library of Victoria
Melbourne, Vic.
Masterplan and first stages of infill
buildings and refurbishment and fitout of
existing buildings

**Lakeside Promenade and Central Area
Light Fittings**
Canberra, ACT

1990

SpineCare Village, Stage 1
Ryde, NSW
Rehabilitation centre

Waterfront House
Vaucluse, NSW
Waterfront residence

**Parliamentary Zone Mall Road,
Stage 2**
Canberra, ACT

1991

Exhibition and Sports Halls
Homebush Bay, NSW
Design for Olympic bid document

Carslaw Building
University of Sydney, NSW
Additions and alterations

MLC School
Burwood, Sydney, NSW
Refurbishment and new classroom
building

Royal Botanic Gardens
Sydney, NSW
Botanical centre

Park Hyatt Hotel
Campbells Cove, NSW
Alterations

1992

Sydney Airport Control Tower
Sydney Airport, NSW

Blood Bank and Laboratories
Parramatta, NSW
Blood donor laboratory and distribution
centre

Skydeer Park Retirement Community
Guangzhou, China
Retirement housing (unbuilt)

Sand River, Shenzhen
Shenzhen, China
Golf and country club resort and housing

South Pacific Commission
Noumea, New Caledonia
43 dwellings and apartments and
associated infrastructure

Singapore Hotel
Orchard Road, Singapore
Development tender submission

Wentworth Student Union Building, Stage 3
University of Sydney, NSW

RAS Master Plan for Olympic Bid Document
Homebush Bay, NSW

1993

Nowra Administrative Centre
Nowra, NSW
Administration offices

Powerhouse Museum
Haymarket, NSW
Property development plan

Novar Street
Yarralumla, ACT
Brian Pettit
Dual occupancy residence

Pettit House
14 The Greenway, Terrey Hills, NSW
Single residence

SpineCare Village, Stage 3
Ryde, NSW
Rehabilitation centre

Garvan Institute of Medical Research
St Vincent's Hospital, Darlinghurst, NSW
Laboratory for medical and experimental research

1994

The Education Building
Bridge Street, Sydney, NSW
Heritage restoration work and refurbishment of office space

Bushell's Building
Sydney, NSW
Conference centre; development tender for CRI

1995

Laboratory for Surgical and Experimental Research
Westmead, NSW
Masterplan and siting study

Olympic Multi-Use Arena Studies for SOCOG
Homebush Bay, NSW

Gateway Light Rail Station
Pyrmont, NSW
Design advice and controls for new station

Park Hyatt Hotel
Campbells Cove, NSW
Alterations to north windows and balconies

Willock Street and Central Road
Miranda, NSW
Apartment buildings

Walsh Bay
NSW
Refurbished finger wharves, hotel, apartments and concert hall; development tender submission for CRI

1996

Go Var
Ho Chi Minh City, Vietnam
50 row houses project

State Hockey Centre
Homebush Bay, NSW
For 2000 Olympic Games

Town Hall House Offices
Kent Street, Sydney, NSW
New entrance and refurbishment

Tuggerah Public School
Tuggerah, NSW

Ourimbah Public School
Ourimbah, NSW

The Pier
589 New South Head Road, Rose Bay, NSW
3 overlapping townhouses

Royal Agricultural Showground Exhibition Halls and Administration Building
Homebush Bay, NSW
Dome and indoor sports facility for 2000 Olympic Games

1997

Macquarie University Library Extension and Cogeneration Plant
Ryde, NSW

Hill Road Car Park Amenities
Homebush Bay, NSW

Jersey Road Apartments
Jersey Road, Woollahra, NSW

State Library of Victoria
Master plan review

1998

Park Hyatt Hotel
Campbells Cove, NSW
New restaurant

Sydney Convention Centre
Darling Harbour, Sydney, NSW
Convention building

Harry House
50 George Street
East Melbourne, Vic.

State Library of Victoria, Stage 4 and Stage 5
Melbourne, Vic.
And temporary National Gallery of Victoria fitout

Awards, Competitions and Exhibitions

Awards and Competitions

Sulman Award
Royal Australian Institute of Architects
Ancher House, Killara, NSW
1945

Research Bursary
Board of Architects
Stuart Murray
1949

Travelling Scholarship
Byera Hadley
Bryce Mortlock
1951

Travelling Scholarship
Byera Hadley
Ken Woolley
1955

University Medal, Sulman Medal & First Class Honours
University of Sydney, NSW
Ken Woolley
1955

First Prize
Waverly Town Hall Competition
Stuart Murray
1958

First Prize
Taubmans Australian House Competition
Ken Woolley & Michael Dysart
1958

Sulman Award
Royal Australian Institute of Architects
House at Dolans Bay Rd, Cronulla, NSW
Bryce Mortlock
1961

Wilkinson Award
Royal Australian Institute of Architects
House at Bullecourt Avenue, Mosman, NSW
Ken Woolley
1962

Sulman Award & RIBA Bronze Medal
Royal Australian Institute of Architects
Fisher Library, University of Sydney
Camperdown, NSW
Joint architects: The Government
Architect, E.H. Farmer & T.E. O'Mahony
Ken Woolley, design architect for the
Government Architect
1962

Award Winner
Sunday Telegraph Small House Design
Competition
1964

Project House Design Award
(Low Cost Category)
Royal Australian Institute of Architects
Pettit & Sevitt house
1967

Blacket Award for Country Buildings
Royal Australian Institute of Architects
University of Newcastle Student Union
Newcastle, NSW
1967

First Prize, Limited Competition
Great Hall, University of Newcastle
Newcastle, NSW
1968

Highly Commended
National Gallery, Canberra
Second place in limited competition
1968

Project House Design Award
(Medium Cost Category)
Royal Australian Institute of Architects
Pettit & Sevitt house
1968

Project House Award
The Age (Melbourne)
Pettit & Sevitt house
1968

Western Australia Project House Awards
(Three categories awarded)
Royal Australian Institute of Architects
Three Project Houses for Corser Homes
Perth, WA
1968

ACI St Regis Scholarship
Ken Woolley
1968

Wilkinson Award
Royal Australian Institute of Architects
The Penthouses, Darling Point, NSW
1969

Project House Design Award
(Low Cost Category)
Royal Australian Institute of Architects
Pettit & Sevitt house
1969

Project House Design Award
(Medium Cost Category)
Royal Australian Institute of Architects
Pettit & Sevitt house
1969

Blacket Award for Country Buildings
Royal Australian Institute of Architects
Staff House, University of Newcastle
Newcastle, NSW
1969

Project House Design Award
(Low Cost Category)
Royal Australian Institute of Architects
Pettit & Sevitt house
1970

Project House Design Award
(Medium Cost Category)
Royal Australian Institute of Architects
Pettit & Sevitt house
1970

Merit Award
Royal Australian Institute of Architects
Wentworth Student Union Building,
University of Sydney
1972

Merit Award, Housing
Royal Australian Institute of Architects
Mosman Townhouses
Almora Street, Mosman, NSW
Bryce Mortlock
1972

Project House Design Award
(Medium Cost Category)
Royal Australian Institute of Architects
Pettit & Sevitt house
1973

Project House Design Award
(Medium Cost Category)
Royal Australian Institute of Architects
Pettit & Sevitt house
1974

Winner, Limited Competition
100 Townhouses and Village Centre
Holsworthy, NSW
1976

Gold Medal
Royal Australian Institute of Architects
Sydney Ancher
1976

Merit Award, Housing
Royal Australian Institute of Architects
108 Group Houses
Macquarie Fields, NSW
1976

Project House Design Award
(Medium Cost Category)
Royal Australian Institute of Architects
Pettit & Sevitt house
1976

Project House Design Award
(Medium Cost Category)
Royal Australian Institute of Architects
Pettit & Sevitt house
1976

Project House Design Award
(Medium Cost Category)
Royal Australian Institute of Architects
Pettit & Sevitt house
1976

Bathurst Orange Housing Competition
Second prize in two-stage competition
1978

Merit Award
Royal Australian Institute of Architects
Sydney Square (other than St Andrew's
House, Town Hall House and Town Hall)
Sydney, NSW
In collaboration with Noel Bell-Ridley
Smith Architects
1978

Winner, Limited Competition
Australian Institute of Criminology
Canberra, ACT
1979

Merit Award
Royal Australian Institute of Architects
Sydney Town Hall Complex
Sydney, NSW
1979

Gold Medal
Royal Australian Institute of Architects
Bryce Mortlock
1979

Winner, Limited Competition
Linley Cove Housing Development
Lane Cove, NSW
1980

Merit Award
Botanic Gardens Kiosk
Sydney, NSW
With NSW Government Architect
1980

Merit Award, Conservation Category
Royal Australian Institute of Architects
Building conversion for the NSW Nurses
Association
Darlinghurst, NSW
1980

Bronze Medal
Royal Australian Institute of Architects,
Victoria Chapter
Environmental design of Melbourne
University complex
Bryce Mortlock
1981

Merit Award
Royal Australian Institute of Architects
Woolley House, Paddington, NSW
1981

Merit Award
Royal Australian Institute of Architects
West Amenities and Project Control
Facility
Garden Island Naval Dockyard, Sydney,
NSW
1982

Order of Australia
Bryce Mortlock
1982

Winner, Limited Competition
National Archives, Canberra, ACT
1983

RAIA Ideas Competition Winner
Royal Australian Institute of Architects
The Quay Gateway
Circular Quay, Sydney, NSW
1983

Wilkinson Award
Royal Australian Institute of Architects
Woolley House, Paddington, NSW
1983

Civic Design Award
Royal Australian Institute of Architects
Sydney Square and Wall of Water
Sydney, NSW
In collaboration with Noel Bell-Ridley
Smith, Architects and Robert Woodward
1983

Highly Commended, BHP Steel Awards
West Amenities and Project Control
Facility
Guided Missile Launching System
Assembly and Overhaul Building
Garden Island Naval Dockyard, Sydney,
NSW
1983

Merit Award for Housing
(CS Daley Housing Category)
Royal Australian Institute of Architects,
ACT Chapter
Yarralumla Shores
Yarralumla, Canberra, ACT
In collaboration with Steve Thomas
1984

Merit Award
Royal Australian Institute of Architects
Mormon Chapel
Railway Parade, Leura, NSW
1984

Winner, Limited Competition
Victorian State Library and Museum
Melbourne, Vic.
1985

Merit Award
Royal Australian Institute of Architects
Guided Missile Launching System
Assembly and Overhaul Building
Garden Island Naval Dockyard, Sydney,
NSW
1985

Winner, Limited Competition
The Australian Hellenic War Memorial
Anzac Parade, Canberra, ACT
1986

Canberra Medallion
Royal Australian Institute of Architects,
ACT Chapter
Australian Defence Force Academy
Cadets Mess
Campbell, ACT
Joint Architects with Department of
Housing and Construction
1986

Sir Zelman Cowen Award
Royal Australian Institute of Architects
National Awards
Australian Defence Force Academy
Cadets Mess
Campbell, ACT
Joint Architects with Department of
Housing and Construction
1986

Winner, Development Competition
Campbells Cove site
Circular Quay, Sydney, NSW
1987

Wilkinson Award
Royal Australian Institute of Architects
Woolley House, Palm Beach, NSW
1987

Robin Boyd Award
Royal Australian Institute of Architects
National Awards
Woolley House, Palm Beach, NSW
1987

Blacket Award for Country Buildings
Royal Australian Institute of Architects,
NSW Country Division
The Anchorage
Tweed Heads, NSW
1987

Wingecarribee Shire Design Award
Community and Civic Improvements,
Corbett Plaza
Bowral, NSW
1987

Winner, Development Competition
Walsh Bay Foreshore Development
Walsh Bay, Sydney, NSW
1988

Order of Australia
Ken Woolley, for services to architecture
1988

**Winner, Cumberland Street Site
Development Competition**
Sydney Cove Authority
1989

Winner, Development Competition
Darling Harbour, East Esplanade
Sydney, NSW
1989

Australian Airlines Business Award
Best Commercial or Office Building
City of Liverpool
Liverpool Town Centre
Liverpool, NSW
1989

BHP Steel Merit Award
"The Arc" Glasshouses
Royal Botanic Gardens, Sydney, NSW
1990

Winner, Limited Competition
Royal Botanic Gardens Centre
Sydney, NSW
1991

Civic Design Merit Award
Royal Australian Institute of Architects
Park Hyatt Hotel
Campbells Cove, NSW
1991

Merit Award for Architecture
Royal Australian Institute of Architects
ABC Radio and Orchestra Centre
Ultimo, Sydney, NSW
1992

Merit Award for Architecture
Royal Australian Institute of Architects
Children's Medical Research Institute
Westmead, Sydney, NSW
1993

Gold Medal
Royal Australian Institute of Architects
Ken Woolley
1993

Finalist, BHP Australian Steel Awards
Sydney Airport Control Tower
Sydney Airport, NSW
1995

High Commendation, Architectural Steel Design Award for Buildings
Australian Institute of Steel Construction
NSW
Sydney Airport Control Tower
Sydney Airport, NSW
1995

Twenty-Five Year Award
Royal Australian Institute of Architects,
ACT Chapter
Seventh Day Adventist Church
Turner, Canberra, ACT
1996

Exhibitions

EXPO Montreal
Woolley House, Mosman, NSW
Ken Woolley
Montreal, Canada
1967

Sulman & Wilkinson Awards Exhibition
Royal Australian Institute of Architects
Sydney, NSW
1963

RAIA Members Exhibition
Royal Australian Institute of Architects
Sydney, NSW
1964

RAIA Awards Exhibitions
Royal Australian Institute of Architects
Sydney, NSW
1968–1982

EXPO Tokyo
Woolley House, Mosman; Macquarie
University Student Union Building, North
Ryde; The Penthouses, Darling Point,
NSW
Tokyo, Japan
1970

Retrospective Exhibition: 30 years of Ancher Mortlock Murray & Woolley
Art Gallery of New South Wales
Sydney, NSW
1976

RAIA Australian Architecture Touring Exhibition
Royal Australian Institute of Architects
1977

Exhibition on the Preservation of Engehurst
Royal Australian Institute of Architects
Pleasures of Architecture Conference
University of Technology, Sydney, NSW
1980

RAIA Convention Exhibition
Royal Australian Institute of Architects
Competition for the Quay
Regent Hotel, Sydney, NSW
1983

International Travelling Exhibition: "Old Continent New Building"
Royal Australian Institute of Architects
1983–1985

Triennale of World Architecture Exhibition
Belgrade, Yugoslavia
1985

"Australian Architects, Ken Woolley" Book Exhibition
Art Gallery of New South Wales
Sydney, NSW
1985

Australian Built, "Responding to the Place" Exhibition
Art Gallery of New South Wales
Sydney, NSW
1985

Competition Exhibition
Victorian State Library and Museum
Melbourne, Vic.
1986

Australia by Design Exhibition
Powerhouse Museum
Sydney, NSW
1987

RAIA Awards Exhibitions
Sydney, NSW
1987–1993

Sydney Harbour Foreshore Development Exhibition
Royal Australian Institute of Architects
Sydney, NSW
1989

Exhibition of Australian Design Excellence,
Australian Academy of Design and
Department of Foreign Affairs
Manila, The Philippines and South East
Asia
1992

Design of the 50s Exhibition
Powerhouse Museum
Sydney, NSW
1993

Bibliography

Articles

"1993 Architecture Awards Winners: Merit Award: Public Buildings." *Architecture Bulletin* (July 1993), p. 9. (Children's Medical Research Institute)

"1993 Children's Medical Research Institute." *Architecture Australia* (vol. 82, no. 5, September–October 1993), pp. 32–33.

"ABC Radio and Orchestra Headquarters, Ultimo." *Architecture Bulletin* (August 1991), pp. 4–6. (Architect's statement)

"ABC Radio and Orchestral Complex." *Constructional Review* (vol. 65, no. 1, February 1992) pp. 6–13.

Allenby, Guy. "Tower de Force." *Corporate Office Design* (vol. 2, no. 1, Autumn–Winter 1995), pp. 66–68. (Sydney Airport Control Tower)

"Ancher Mortlock & Woolley: Office at 93 George Street, Parramatta." *Architecture Australia* (vol. 76, no. 6, September 1987), pp. 97–98.

"Ancher Mortlock and Woolley: Two Recent Projects from Ancher Mortlock & Woolley: A Residential Development at Tweed Heads on the Gold Coast and an Office Development in Sydney." *Architecture Australia* (vol. 76, no. 6, September 1987), pp. 94–98.

"The Anchorage, Tweed Heads." *Builder NSW* (vol. 15, no. 9, October 1986), pp. 508–514.

"The Anchorage." *Builder NSW* (vol. 17, no. 3, April 1988), pp. 164–171.

"Architect's Own House, Mosman, Australia." *Architecture in Australia* (no. 52, December 1963), pp. 76–83.

"Architect's Own Townhouse, Paddington." *Builder NSW* (vol. 12, no. 10, November 1983), pp. 722–724. (Woolley House, Paddington)

"Australian Architecture 1992." *Design Ink* (no. 8, March 1992), pp. 12–13. (ABC Radio and Orchestra Centre; Park Hyatt Hotel; Glasshouses, Royal Botanic Gardens; Commonwealth Law Courts)

Australian Building, Construction and Housing (vol. 27, no. 4, May 1997), p. 30. (RAS Exhibition Halls)

"Award Winning Buildings, Australia, 1967–1968." *Architecture in Australia* (vol. 57, no. 6, November 1968) pp. 923–957. (University of Newcastle Student Union)

"Awards for Building 1984." *Builder NSW* (no. 10, November 1984), pp. 682, 691–692. (Mormon Chapel, Leura)

"Awards for Buildings 1987: Woolley House, Palm Beach, Sydney." *Builder NSW* (vol. 16, no. 10, November 1987), pp. 652–656.

"Awards/84: Merit Award 1984." *Architecture Bulletin* (no. 10, October 1984), p. 7. (Review)

"Awards: 1983 Wilkinson Award." *Architecture Bulletin* (October 1983), p. 4. (Woolley House, Paddington)

Beck, Haig. "Ken Woolley Gold." *Architecture Australia* (vol. 82, no. 5, September–October 1993), pp. 28–31. (30 selected buildings)

Blueprint (UK, November 1989), p. 18. (Walsh Bay, Campbells Cove)

Brennan, Betsy. "The Australian Pavilion, Expo 1988." *Vogue Living* (vol. 22, no. 8, October 1988), pp. 118–121.

Brewer, Colin. "Timber—New Applications." *Builder NSW* (vol. 17, no. 1, February 1988), pp. 43–44.

Browne, Kenneth. "Sydney Square." *Architectural Review* (UK, February 1980).

Browne, Kenneth. "The Penthouses." *Architectural Review* (UK, 1981).

Builder NSW (vol. 14, no. 10, November 1985), pp. 658–665 (Mormon Chapel, Leura), 666, 676 (GMLS Building, Garden Island).

Building Construction Materials & Equipment (vol. 28, no. 10, February–March 1987), pp. 215. (Australian Defence Forces Academy Cadets Mess)

Building Innovation and Construction Technology (no. 16, June–July 1997), pp. 30–31. (RAS Exhibition Halls)

Building Services Australia (December 1990–January 1991), p. 234. (ABC Radio and Orchestra Centre)

"Categories 5, 6, 7 Nominations: Merit Awards 1983." *Architecture Bulletin* (August 1983) pp. 16–17. (The Corso, Manly)

"Category 3 Nominations: Merit Awards 1983." *Architecture Bulletin* (July 1983), pp. 16–17. (Linley Cove Housing Development)

"Chapel for the Church of Jesus Christ of Latter Day Saints, Leura" and "Yarralumla Shores". *Architecture Australia* (vol. 73, no. 8, December 1984), pp. 23, 44.

"Commonwealth Law Courts." *Constructional Review* (vol. 64, no. 2, May 1991), pp. 8–15.

"Control Tower, Sydney Airport." *Monument* (no. 11, 1996), pp. 28–29.

"Courtyard Houses at Cremorne, N.S.W." *The Australian Journal of Architecture and Arts* (vol. 15, no. 7, July 1967) p. 17. (The Cottages)

Day, Norman. "Sydney's Haut Gout: The High Flavoured Taste." *Architecture Australia* (vol. 71, no. 1, January 1982), pp. 27–33. (Woolley House, Paddington)

Devenish, John. "Woolloomooloo Townscape: An Exercise in Controlled Diversity." *Architecture Australia* (vol. 70, no. 4, September 1981), pp. 55–63. (Housing Commission row houses)

Dickinson, Michael. "The Changing Australian Home." *National Times* (8–14 February 1981), pp. 31–32.

"The Eighth Wonder." *Architecture Australia* (vol. 85, no. 1, January–February 1996). (Review by Ken Woolley of performance in the Sydney Opera House, 14 October – 4 November 1995)

Evans, Michael. "Hockey Set Gets a Jolly Along." *Sydney Morning Herald* (Friday 28 August 1998), p. 16. (State Hockey Centre)

"Excellence in Construction Awards 1989: Glasshouse Complex, Royal Botanic Gardens, Sydney." *Australian Building Construction & Housing* (vol. 18, no. 10, November 1989), pp. 578–581.

"Excellence in Construction Awards 1990: Park Hyatt on Sydney Harbour Hotel, Campbell's Cove." *Australian Building, Construction & Housing* (vol. 19, no. 10, November 1990), pp. 590–592. (Park Hyatt Hotel)

"Excellence in Housing Awards 1985: Home Units Lend Lease Homes Pty Ltd." *Builder NSW* (vol. 14, no. 9, October 1985), pp. 538, 560, 562, 564–565. (Linley Cove Housing Development)

"Exhibition Village at St Ives, N.S.W. Pettit and Sevitt." *The Australian Journal of Architecture and Arts* (vol. 14, no. 11, November 1966), pp. 13–15.

Farrelly, E.M. "Are the 60's Worth Saving?" *Sydney Morning Herald* (7 February 1996). (State Office Block)

Farrelly, E.M. "Design Versus Dollars: The Hyatt at Campbell's Cove: Ancher Mortlock & Woolley." *Architecture Bulletin* (June 1989), p. 4.

Farrelly, E.M. "What Would You Save?" *Sydney Morning Herald* (Tuesday 7 January 1997), p. 28. (Fisher Library; State Office Block)

"F.C. Pye Field Environment Laboratory." *Building* (212: 26, 30 June 1967) pp. 69–70.

"Feature: Roofing: Roof Steels Attention." *Building Construction Materials & Equipment* (vol. 32, no. 6, number 208, August 1990), p. 28. (Steel roof, Park Hyatt Hotel)

Fiorentini, Frank et al. "Ken Woolley." *Critiques* (Parkville, Victoria, vol. 1, 1987), pp. 144, 169.

"First Six Star Property To Boast Historical Setting." *Australian* (20 February 1987), p. 18. (Park Hyatt Hotel)

Fitzhardinge, Richard and Andrew Young. "Current Domestic Architecture in Sydney." *Architectural Design* (UK, August 1964), pp. 406–407. (Woolley House, Mosman)

Fortescue, Elizabeth. "Facelift for a Flawed Beauty." *Daily Telegraph* (Monday 5 August 1996), p. 4. (Comment by Ken Woolley on the city centre)

Freeland, Max. "A Plan for Future Living: Modern Australian Architecture." *National Times* (18 September 1972). (Woolley House, Mosman; Sydney Town Hall Complex; Pettit & Sevitt Houses; BHP Steel House; Milson Road Townhouses; statement by Ken Woolley on the emergence of the Sydney School)

"From Federation to Today: The 1960s—The Sydney School." *Belle* (no. 67, January–February 1985), p. 95.

"The Gardens Restaurant." *Builder NSW* (September 1980), pp. 460–465.

Gordon, Douglas. "Awards: 1983 Civic Design Award." *Architecture Bulletin* (October 1983), p. 5. (Sydney Square and wall of water fountain)

"Homebush Bay and the Green Olympics." *Australian Building, Construction & Housing* (vol. 27, no. 5, 1997) pp. 14–17.

"House at Cronulla, NSW, Australia." *International Asbestos-Cement Review* (20: 2, no. 78, April 1974), pp. 50–51.

"House at Middle Cove." *The Australian Journal of Architecture and Arts* (vol. 15, no. 1, January 1967), pp. 12–13. (Baudish House, Middle Cove)

Hughes, Anthony. "Plans for State Office Block Spark Row." *Sydney Morning Herald* (4 June 1996), p. 30. (Demolition of State Office Block)

Hyatt, Peter. "Tower of Power." *Steel Profile* (no. 51, March 1995), pp. 13–17. (Sydney Airport Control Tower)

"In the News: 25 Year Award to Ken Woolley." *Architecture Bulletin* (November 1997), p. 2. (Seventh Day Adventist Church, Canberra)

"Innovative Features of the Australian Embassy in Bangkok." *Asian Building and Construction* (May 1977), pp. 25–29.

"Interview with Ken Woolley: The Context of the Melbourne/Sydney Debate." *Transition: Discourse on Architecture* (no. 21, September 1987), pp. 13–22.

Jackson, Davina & Zinta Jurjans. "Showcase: Interior Motives." *Belle* (no. 93, June–July 1989), pp. 41–48.

James, Col. "Gateway to More." *Architecture Bulletin* (January–February 1983), pp. 9–12. (The Gateway Competition, winning scheme)

Jiminez, Cathryn. "Dome To Star at Olympic Site." *Australian Financial Review* (23 October 1996), p. 33.

Keens, Leta. "Simply a Weekender." *Belle* (vol. 86, April–May 1988), pp. 66–73. (Woolley House, Palm Beach)

Kelly, William with Ken Woolley and Neville Quarry (eds). *NOW: Architectural and Building News of the World* (August 1967).

Keniger, Michael. "Olympics Showground." *Architecture Australia* (vol. 86, no. 3, May–June 1997), pp. 76–79. (RAS Exhibition Halls)

"Ken Woolley's Distinguished Career." *Architecture Australia* (vol. 82, no. 5, September–October 1993), pp. 34–35.

"Ken Woolley: Winner of the Gold Medal 1993." Text of speech delivered by Ken Woolley as gold medal winner. *Architecture Bulletin* (October 1993), pp. 16–17, 19.

"Laboratory Conditions." *Corporate and Office Design* (vol. 9, no. 2, 1993), pp. 68–71. (Children's Medical Research Institute)

"Laboratory: F.C. Pye Field Environment Laboratory, Canberra." *Architecture in Australia* (vol. 58, no. 3, June 1969), pp. 497–502.

Lawson, Sylvia. "ABC Pushed for a Single Purpose Hall." Letter to the editor. *Australian* (Friday 2 June 1995). (Sydney Opera House)

Lukas, Isobel. "From Chic Townhouse to Lavish Embassy." *Sydney Morning Herald* (28 November 1984), p. 12. (Interview with Ken Woolley)

Mathison, Colin and Peter Thompson. "Vanuatu Broadcasting Services Project." *Arup Journal* (UK, vol. 16, no. 4, December 1981), pp. 11–13.

McDougall, Ian, Ken Woolley, Peter Myers, Conrad Hamann and Sue Dance. "Transition 1982 Competition Results." *Transition* 3 (3–4, April–July 1984), pp. 43–55.

McDougall, Ian. "The International Hotel: Interview with Ken Woolley, Architect of the Park Hyatt Hotel." *Architecture Australia* (vol. 80, no. 3, April 1991), pp. 40–42. (Campbells Cove, Sydney)

"Merit Award Section 1: West Wharf Amenities and Refit Building, Garden Island." *Architecture Australia* (vol. 71, no. 6, December 1982), pp. 22–23.

"Merit Award Section 2: Woolley House, Paddington." *Architecture Australia* (vol. 70, no. 6, December 1982), pp. 26–27.

Morris, Linda. "Happy Landings at Last for New Airport Tower." *Sydney Morning Herald* (24 July 1996), p. 3.

Mould, Peter. "Going to Court: Two Family Courts Retreat from Informality." *Architecture Australia* (May 1994), pp. 6–11. (Commonwealth Law Courts)

"Our Paving is Crazy." *Daily Telegraph* (Thursday 8 August 1996), p. 14. (Statement by Ken Woolley)

Osborne, Catherine. "Corporate Headquarters: ABC Ultimo Centre." *Corporate and Office Design* (vol. 8, no. 4, 1992), pp. 134–139.

"Park Hyatt Hotel." *Constructional Review* (vol. 6, no. 4, November 1990), pp. 10–17.

Pegrum, Roger. "Architectural Details: Assembly and Overhaul Building, Garden Island." *Architecture Australia* (vol. 75, no. 1, January 1986), pp. 24–29. (GMLS Building, Garden Island)

"Prestige Hotels and Convention Centres." *Sydney Morning Herald* (24 April 1987). (Proposed hotel for Campbells Cove)

Proudfoot, Peter. "Another Landmark Hole!" Letter to the editor. *Sydney Morning Herald* (Wednesday 27 November 1996). (State Office Block)

"Radio and Orchestra Facility, Sydney." *Constructional Review* (vol. 61, no. 4, November 1988), p. 4.

"RAIA Awards 1987: The Robin Boyd Award for Residential Works." *Architecture Australia* (vol. 76, no. 8, December 1987), pp. 60–65. (Woolley House, Palm Beach)

"Recent Buildings." *Architecture in Australia* (vol. 58, no. 4, August 1969), pp. 617–620 (The Penthouses), 629–632 (The Cottages), 643–646 (Pettit & Sevitt Split Level Mark 1E, 2E).

"Recent Domestic Architecture, Australia." *Architecture in Australia* (vol. 60, no. 1, February 1971), pp. 21–69. (Myers House, Mosman)

"Recycled Building." *Builder NSW* (vol. 10, no. 3, April 1981), pp. 150–157. (NSW Nurses Association)

"Review of *Australian Architects: Ken Woolley.*" *TAS: The Architecture Show* (October 1986).

Robertson, H.H. "Garden Island Dockyard." *The Architecture Show* (NSWIT, December 1984), pp. 42–43.

Sandeman, John. "Architects Blend Old and New in Award Designs." *National Times* (8–14 November 1981), pp. 20–21.

Saunders, David. "Modern Australian Architecture." *Process Architecture* (Tokyo, no. 22, March 1981), whole issue. (Woolley House, Mosman; The Penthouses; Sydney Town Hall Complex)

Schofield, Leo. "A Moving Experience." *Sydney Morning Herald* (Saturday 11 April 1998). (Walsh Bay tendering process; State Office Block)

"Showground Exhibition Halls." *Architecture Australia* (vol. 85, no. 6, November–December 1996), p. 18.

"The Sir Zelman Cowan Award for Non-Residential Works." *Architecture Australia* (vol. 75, no. 8, December 1986), pp. 22–25. (Australian Defence Forces Academy Cadets Mess)

"Sliding Scale for Good Architecture." *Sydney Morning Herald* (22 July 1996), p. 13. (Olympic plans, including RAS Exhibition Halls)

Smith, Vincent. "The Battle of Victoria Street: Development Projects by Stephenson & Turner, Rommel Moorcroft, Ken Woolley, and Neville Gruzman." *Architecture in Australia* (vol. 65, no. 3, June–July 1976), pp. 36–45.

Staas, Robert. "The Real Sydney Style." *Mosman Daily* (28 May 1998), p. 19.

"The Staff House, University of Newcastle, NSW." *Architecture in Australia* (vol. 60, no. 2, April 1971), pp. 214–219.

"State Library Speaks Volumes about Melbourne's Architectural Revolution." *Age* (7 October 1995). (State Library of Victoria)

"Student Union Building, Macquarie University, Eastwood, North Ryde, Australia." *Architecture + Urbanism* (Japan, vol. 2, no. 6, June 1972), pp. 52–55.

"Students' Centre of Sydney University." *Detail* (Munich, no. 6, November–December 1973), pp. 120–120.

"Survey 3: Airport Control Tower." *Constructional Review* (vol. 66, no. 4, November 1993), p. 8.

"Survey: State Library and Museum." *Constructional Review* (vol. 59, no. 2, May 1986), p. 3.

Susskind, Anne. "A House Divided." *Sydney Morning Herald* (Saturday 10 February 1996). (Sydney Opera House)

Susskind, Anne. "Architect Mourns as Building Waits To Topple." *Sydney Morning Herald* (2 September 1996). (State Office Block)

Susskind, Anne. "Home of the Dome." *Sydney Morning Herald* (Friday 3 April 1998), p. 19. (RAS Exhibition Halls)

"Sydney Square, Including the Water Fountain." *Builder NSW* (vol. 12, no. 10, 1983), pp. 724–726.

"Sydney Square." *Architecture Australia* (vol. 67, no. 6, January 1979), p. 391.

"Sydney Town Hall Complex." *Builder NSW* (June 1980), pp. 278–286.

"Sydney's New ABC Building." *Building Economist* (December 1992), pp. 33–36.

Tanner, Howard. "ABC Centre a Media Palace." *Architecture Bulletin* (August 1991), pp. 7–9.

Taylor, Jennifer. "Looking at the Sydney School." *Transition* (vol. 1, no. 2, November 1979), pp. 4–8. (Woolley House, Mosman)

Taylor, Ken. "Anzac Parade: A Landscape of Memory." *Canberra Historical Journal* (no. 38, September 1996) (Australian Hellenic War Memorial)

"Terrassen-hauser." *d-extrakt* (Bonn, 12 April 1973). (The Penthouses)

"Terrassen-Wohnhauser in Sydney, Australien." *Detail* (Munich, no. 5, September–October), pp. 926–928. (The Penthouses)

Thompson, Peter and Peter Haworth. "Australian Embassies." *Arup Journal* (UK, vol. 11, no. 3, October 1976), pp.18–22. (Australian Embassy, Bangkok)

"Timber Dome, Royal Agricultural Showgrounds, Homebush Bay." *Architect* (Victoria, November–December 1997), p. 12.

Totaro, Paola and Robert Wainwright. "Casting a Long Shadow over Quay Development." *Sydney Morning Herald* (Wednesday 11 June 1997), p. 7.

Totaro, Paola and Robert Wainwright. "The Man with the Plan." *Sydney Morning Herald* (Saturday 7 June 1997), p. 38. (East Circular Quay; references to David Brice and Ken Woolley)

Totaro, Paola. "Carr Lifts Wraps off Plan for New $384m Showground." *Sydney Morning Herald* (Wednesday 23 October 1996), p. 2.

Totaro, Paola. "Towering Feelings ... What Is Inspiring Our Architects?" *Sydney Morning Herald* (Saturday 31 May 1997). (Reference to David Brice and Ken Woolley)

Transition 56 (1997), p. 43. (RAS Exhibition Halls)

"Tropical Centre." *Constructional Review* (vol. 64, no. 1, February 1991), pp. 18–25. (Glasshouses, Royal Botanic Gardens)

"Ubereinander gestapelte Penthauser: Wohenlage in Darling Point, Australien." *Baumeister* (Germany, no. 67, February 1970), pp. 142–145. (The Penthouses)

"Union Couple." *Architectural Review* (UK, no. 915, May 1973), pp. 338–339. (Macquarie University Union Building)

"University and College Buildings in Australia." *Architecture in Australia* (vol. 59, no. 2, April 1970), pp. 223–249. (Macquarie University Union Building)

"University of Newcastle in Shortland, Australia." *Baumeister* (Germany, vol. 75, no. 11, November 1978), pp. 976–979.

Veale, Sharon. "Significant Building." *Architecture Bulletin* (June 1996), p. 7. (State Office Block)

"Victorian State Library and Museum Competition: Comment on the Assessment of Entries and the Design Statement of the Winners, Ancher Mortlock and Woolley." *Architecture Bulletin* (April 1986), pp. 8–11, 13–15.

Wainwright, Robert and Paola Totaro. "One Man's $800m Plan To Save the Quay." *Sydney Morning Herald* (Monday 2 June 1997). (East Circular Quay; references to David Brice and Ken Woolley)

Walter, Betsy. "A Class of Their Own." *Belle* (November–December 1981), pp. 48–49. (Woolley House, Paddington)

Ward, Peter. "Show and Tell." *Australian* (Friday 3 April 1998), p. 40. (RAS Exhibition Halls)

"Wentworth Building, Stage 2, City Road and Butlin Ave, Sydney University." *Australian Building Construction & Housing* (vol. 18, no. 8, September 1989), pp. 458–465.

"The Wentworth Building, City Road, University of Sydney." *Architecture in Australia* (vol. 60, no. 4, August 1973), pp. 62–67.

"Wentworth Building, Stage 2." *Constructional Review* (vol. 62, no. 2, May 1989), pp. 34–39.

"West Wharf Amenities and Refit Building, Garden Island, Sydney." *Builder NSW* (vol. 11, no. 10, November 1982), pp. 623–624. (Merit Award jurors' comments)

"West Wharf Amenities and Refit Building." *Architectural Bulletin* (no. 10, 1982), p. 12.

"West Wharf Amenities Building." *Builder NSW* (vol. 12, no. 7, August 1983), pp. 426–433.

Wheatland, Bill. "The Day Hall Spoke of Anguish and Fear." Letter to the editor. *Australian* (30 May 1995). (Sydney Opera House)

"The Winner: Ken Woolley: The Victorian State Library/Museum Competition." *Architect* (Melbourne, April 1986), pp. 6–7.

Wislocki, Peter. "Design Review: Flights of Fancy." *Architectural Review* (UK, July 1996), p. 20. (Sydney Airport Control Tower)

Woolley, Ken, "Architect's Statement, Public Works Comment." *Architecture Bulletin* (October 1995), p. 13. (Public architecture)

Woolley, Ken. "A Matter of Style." Based on a public lecture, given as Visiting Professor at the University of New South Wales, 1983.

Woolley, Ken. "A Nation is Many Places." Paper delivered to the Royal Institute of British Architects, London, April 1987. *Architecture Bulletin* (no. 4, 1987), p. 5.

Woolley, Ken. "Abandoned." Letter to the editor. *Sydney Morning Herald* (15 March 1996). (Utzon's glass wall scheme for Sydney Opera House)

Woolley, Ken. "Ancher Mortlock & Woolley: Australian Archives, Canberra, ACT (1983)" and "Ancher Mortlock & Woolley with NCDC: Police Headquarters Canberra, ACT (1984)." *International Architect* (UIA 4, 1984), pp. 2, 32–33 (Australian Archives, Canberra), 40 (Police Headquarters, Canberra), 60 (biographical statement).

Woolley, Ken. "Architect Rescued the Opera House." *Australian* (Wednesday 24 May 1995), p. 12. (Obituary for Peter Hall)

Woolley, Ken. "Australia's Terrace Houses: Sydney's Ornate Fronts Reflect 19th Century Optimism." *Architectural Forum* (New York, vol. 134, no. 4, May 1971), pp. 46–51.

Woolley, Ken. "Australian Domestic Architecture." *Art and Australia* (vol. 9, no. 1, June 1971).

Woolley, Ken. "Australian Embassy, Bangkok." *Architecture Australia* (vol. 74, no. 2, March 1985), pp. 42–48.

Woolley, Ken. "Australian Houses." Proceedings of TEGLZ First International Conference on Single Family Houses, Copenhagen, 1969.

Woolley, Ken. "Concrete." *Building Science Forum* (June 1970).

Woolley, Ken. "Favourite Buildings—Ken Woolley: Architecture Speaks to Us about Our Culture." *Architecture Bulletin* (March 1991), p. 5.

Woolley, Ken. "Gateway Idea." *Architectural Bulletin* (January–February 1983), p. 13.

Woolley, Ken. "Give Art a Chance." Walter Burley Griffin Memorial Lecture, Canberra, 1997.

Woolley, Ken. "GMLS Building, Garden Island, Sydney." *Domus* (Italy, no. 663, August 1985), pp. 9–11.

Woolley, Ken. "Housing Forms & Densities." Paper presented to the Housing & Regional Development Advisory Council, Deputy Prime Minister and Minister for Housing and Regional Development (14 August 1995), pp. 1–4.

Woolley, Ken. "How Australians Should Be Housed." *Economic Society of Australia Journal* (no. 24, March 1967), pp. 14–24.

Woolley, Ken. "New South Wales Heritage Legislation." *Architecture in Australia* (vol. 67, no. 2, April–May 1978), pp. 73–76.

Woolley, Ken. "On the Golden Triangle." *Domus* (Italy, no. 667, December 1985), pp. 18–21. (Australian Archives, Canberra)

Woolley, Ken. "Order and Chaos." Paper given as part of the Visiting Professor Program, University of Sydney, School of Architecture, 1990.

Woolley, Ken. "Planning Buildings and Facilities for Higher Education" (book review) and "Travel Sketches." *Architecture in Australia* (vol. 65, no. 4, August–September 1976), pp. 68–69.

Woolley, Ken. "Seventh Day Adventist Church Canberra." *Architectural Review* (Australia, Autumn 1998), p. 100.

Woolley, Ken. "State Library and Museum Redevelopment Plans: Ancher Mortlock and Woolley." *Architecture Australia* (vol. 75, no. 5, July 1986), pp. 32–34.

Woolley, Ken. "State of the Art." Edited extract from A.S. Hook memorial address. *Architecture Australia* (vol. 80, no. 1, January–February 1994), pp. 58–59.

Woolley, Ken. "The Architect's Own House." *Architecture Bulletin* (December 1996), p. 13.

Woolley, Ken. "The Architect's Role in Merchant Building." *Building Ideas* (no. 6, March 1967), pp. 12–15.

Woolley, Ken. "The City Dwellers' Dilemma." *The Australian Journal of Architecture and Art* (vol. 15, no. 7, July 1967), p. 16. (Courtyard housing)

Woolley, Ken. "The Completion of Engehurst." *Architecture Australia* (vol. 69, no. 2, April–May 1980) pp. 52–53.

Woolley, Ken. "Utzon's 2 × 1 Just Didn't Go." Letter to the editor. *Australian* (Monday 12 June 1995). (Sydney Opera House)

Woolley, Ken. "What is Architecture?" Talk given at the School of Architecture, University of Sydney (26 March 1990).

Woolley, Ken. "Woolley House." *Architecture Australia* (vol. 73, no. 5, July 1984), pp. 50–51. (Woolley House, Paddington)

Wright, Lance and Kenneth Browne. "Sydney Square." *Architectural Review* (UK, vol. 162, no. 979, September 1978), p. 139.

"Your OZ Embassies: Projects for New Australian Embassies." *Architecture in Australia* (vol. 63, no. 6, December 1974), pp. 62–67. (Australian Embassy, Bangkok)

Books

Ancher Mortlock & Woolley. "State Library and Museum Architectural Competition." Record of the winning design submitted by Ancher Mortlock & Woolley, Architects, February 1986.

Ancher Mortlock & Woolley. "Victoria State Library and Museum." Design report, July 1987.

Apperly, Richard & Peter Lind. *444 Sydney Buildings.* Sydney: Angus & Robertson/ RAIA, 1970. (Guide book to building locations with numerous Woolley examples)

Apperly, Richard, Robert Irving & Peter Reynolds. *A Pictorial Guide to Identifying Australian Architecture: Styles and Forms from 1788 to the Present.* Sydney: Angus & Robertson/Mead & Beckett, 1989.

Archer, John. "Inside the Illusion." In *Building a Nation: A History of the Australian House.* Collins, 1987, p. 215.

Architects and Interior Designers of Australia and New Zealand. Mulgrave, Victoria: Images Publishing Group, 1994, pp. 80–81.

Architects of Australia and New Zealand. Mulgrave, Victoria: Images Publishing Group, 1990, pp. 18–19.

Architects of Australia. Mulgrave, Victoria: Images Publishing Group, 1988, pp. 14–15.

Australian Architects: Ken Woolley. Australian Architect Series. Sydney: RAIA Education Division, 1985.

Australian Design Yearbook. Ferny Creek, Victoria: Design Editorial, 1994, p. 101.

Beck, Haig & Jackie Cooper (eds). *Australian Architects.* London: Union Internationale des Architectes/ International Architect, 1984. (Australian Archives, Canberra; Police Headquarters, Canberra; statement by Ken Woolley)

Boyd, Robin. *Australia's Home: Why Australians Built the Way They Did.* 1st ed. (with epilogue). Harmondsworth: Penguin, 1968, p. 304. (Pettit & Sevitt Houses)

Boyd, Robin. *The Puzzle of Architecture.* Carlton, Victoria: Melbourne University Press, 1965, p. 154 (Woolley House, Mosman; Sea Ranch).

Braden, Virginia (ed.). *Ken Woolley— Drawings.* Sydney: privately printed, 1983.

Details in Architecture: Creative Detailing by Some of the World's Leading Architects. Mulgrave, Victoria: Images Publishing Group, in press, pp. 16–19. (Sydney Airport Control Tower)

Emanuel, Muriel (ed.). *Contemporary Architects.* 3rd ed. New York: St James Press, 1994. (Statement by Ken Woolley; essay by Jennifer Taylor)

Fletcher, Banister. *History of Architecture.* 19th ed. London: Butterworths, 1987. (Woolley House, Mosman; Woolley House, Paddington)

Freeland, John Maxwell. *Architecture in Australia..* Harmondsworth: Pelican/ Penguin, 1968, pp. 307 (Pettit & Sevitt Houses), 311 (State Office Block).

Griffin, Brian. *Laboratory Design Guide.* Oxford: Boston Architectural Press, 1998. (Children's Medical Research Institute; Blood Bank and Laboratories)

Griggs, Michael & Craig McGregor (eds). *Australian Built: A Photographic Exhibition of Recent Australian Architecture.* North Sydney: Design Arts Board of the Australia Council, 1985.

Haskell, John. *Sydney Architecture.* Sydney: UNSW Press, 1997.

Hayes, Babette & April Hershey. *Australian Style.* Sydney: Paul Hamlyn, 1970.

International Architecture Yearbook No. 2. Mulgrave, Victoria: Images Publishing Group, 1996, pp. 248–249. (Sydney Airport Control Tower)

International Architecture Yearbook No. 3. Mulgrave, Victoria: Images Publishing Group, 1997, pp. 168–171. (Blood Bank and Laboratories)

Irving, Robert et al. *The History and Design of the Australian House.* Oxford University Press, 1985. (Pettit & Sevitt Houses; Woolley House, Mosman; townhouses, Sydney area)

Irving, Robert, John Kinstler & Max Dupain. *Fine Houses of Sydney.* Sydney: Methuen, 1982, pp. 182–188. (Woolley House, Paddington; Woolley House, Mosman)

Jahn, Graham. *Contemporary Australian Architecture.* Gordon and Breach Arts International, 1994, pp. 128–132, 160–164.

Jahn, Graham. *Sydney Architecture.* Sydney: The Watermark Press, 1997, pp. 148, 169, 171, 185, 193, 195, 227.

Johnson, Chris (ed.). *The City in Conflict.* Sydney: Law Book Company, 1985. (Design competition for the Gateway, Circular Quay)

Judd, Bruce & John Dean (eds). *Medium Density Housing in Australia.* Canberra: RAIA, 1983. (Statement by Ken Woolley on issues in housing; The Penthouses)

Lee, Tony (ed.). *Building on Tradition: Nine Designs for the Victorian State Library and Museum.* South Melbourne: Emery Vincent Associates, 1986.

Luscombe, Desley & Anne Peden. *Picturing Architecture*. Craftsman House, 1992, pp. 150–151. (Australian Hellenic War Memorial)

Made in Australia: A Source Book of all Things Australian. Richmond, Victoria: William Heinemann Australia/The Watermark Press, 1986. (Pettit & Sevitt Houses; Woolley House, Mosman)

McGregor, Craig, Harry Williamson & David Moore. *In the Making*. Melbourne: Nelson, 1969, pp. 250–251. (Ken Woolley; Myers House, Mosman; Woolley House, Mosman; The Penthouses)

McKay, Ian, Robin Boyd, Hugh Stretton & John Mant. *Living and Partly Living*. Melbourne: Nelson, 1971, pp. 62–67 (Myers House, Mosman), 100–101 (Woolley House, Mosman), 128–129 (Pettit & Sevitt Houses), 162–163 (The Cottages), 164–165 (Townhouses, Wollstonecraft), 166–169 (The Penthouses).

Mladjenovic, Ivica. "The Work of Ken Woolley." In *Fifty Outstanding Architects of the World*. Belgrade: Institut Gosa, 1984. Also published in *Nas Dom* magazine. (Woolley House, Paddington)

Morrison, Francesca. *Sydney: A Guide to Recent Architecture*. London: Ellipsis, 1997.

Paroissien, Leon & Michael Griggs (eds). *Old Continent New Building: Contemporary Australian Architecture*. Sydney: David Ell/ Design Arts Committee of the Australia Council, 1983, pp. 56–57 (Woolley House, Paddington), 95 (Australian Institute of Criminology, Canberra), 95–96 (Mormon Chapel, Leura), 102 (Kiosk, Royal Botanic Gardens).

Pegrum, Roger. *Details in Australian Architecture*. Vol. 1. Canberra: RAIA Education Division, 1984, pp. 46–47 (Woolley House, Mosman), 62–63 (The Penthouses), 74–75 (Woolley House, Paddington).

Pegrum, Roger. *Details in Australian Architecture*. Vol. 2. Canberra: RAIA Education Division, 1987. (GMLS Building, Garden Island)

Quarry, Neville. *Award Winning Australian Architecture*. Sydney: Craftsman House/ G & B Arts International, 1997, pp. 30–31 (Australian Defence Forces Academy Cadets Mess), 70–71 (Woolley House, Palm Beach).

Saunders, David & Catherine Burke. *Ancher, Mortlock, Murray & Woolley: Sydney Architects 1946–1976*. Sydney: Power Institute of Fine Arts, University of Sydney, 1976.

Schelling, Samantha. *Moving the Showground Home: A Commemorative Look at the Building of Sydney Showground*. Sydney: Olympic Co-ordination Authority, April 1998.

Sowden, Harry. *Towards an Australian Architecture*. Sydney: Ure Smith, 1968, pp. 24–41. (University of Newcastle Student Union; project housing; Woolley House, Mosman; Engineering Precinct, University of Sydney)

Tanner, Howard. *Australian Housing in the Seventies*. Sydney: Ure Smith, 1976, pp. 85 (The Penthouses), 94–95 (Apartment Block, Elizabeth Bay), 86, 96–97 (Town Houses, Cremorne), 117 (proposed townhouses at Rooty Hill for Housing Commission of NSW), 120–121 (Holsworthy, NSW, housing project).

Taylor, Jennifer. *An Australian Identity: Houses for Sydney 1953–63*. Sydney: Department of Architecture, University of Sydney, 1972.

Taylor, Jennifer. *An Australian Identity: Houses for Sydney 1953–63*. 2nd ed. Sydney: Department of Architecture, University of Sydney, 1984.

Taylor, Jennifer. *Australian Architecture Since 1960*. 1st ed. Sydney: Law Book Company, 1986.

Taylor, Jennifer. *Australian Architecture Since 1960*. 2nd ed. Red Hill, ACT: RAIA Education Division, 1990, pp. 23, 29, 39, 40, 43, 46, 47, 62, 63, 66, 88, 105, 106, 143, 200–202, 214, 235.

Taylor, Jennifer. *Tall Buildings in Australian Cities: The Multistoried Office Building 1945–1970*. In press. (State Office Block)

Transport Spaces: A Pictorial Review. Mulgrave, Victoria: Images Publishing Group, in press, pp. 8–9. (Sydney Airport Control Tower)

Water Spaces of the World. Vol. 1. Mulgrave, Victoria: Images Publishing Group, 1997, pp. 174, 175. (Private residence, Vaucluse, Sydney)

Willis, Anne Marie & Cameron Tonkin. *Timber in Context: A Guide to Sustainable Use*. Natspec Guide Series. Sydney: Construction Information Systems, in press.

"Woolley, Ken." In *Contemporary Architects*, edited by Muriel Emanuel. London: Macmillan Press, 1980, pp. 896–898. (Statement by Ken Woolley and short essay by Philip Drew)

"Woolley, Ken." In *Contemporary Architects*. 2nd ed. London: St James Press, 1987. (Essay by Jennifer Taylor; statement by Ken Woolley)

Woolley, Ken. "Sydney Square a Civic Place for the City." In *The Design of Sydney—Three Decades of Change in the City Centre*. Sydney: Law Book Company, 1988.

World Architecture: A Critical Mosaic, 1900–2000. Beijing: The Architectural Society of China/Colombia University, N.Y., in press. (Woolley House, Mosman)

Acknowledgments

Thanks and acknowledgment to Amy Drew and Gloria Meyer who assembled all the material for this book.

The many specialist, services and structural consultants who have been involved in the major projects of the practice are too numerous to mention, but particular acknowledgment is owed to the structural engineers Ove Arup & Partners, Taylor Thomson & Whitting and Connell Wagner for offering structural possibilities which are so often the touchstone for creative architecture concepts.

Special acknowledgment also to Henry and Roger Schimek who built four of the houses in which I have lived.

As it would be impossible to list all the people who have played a part in the work of Ken Woolley and Ancher Mortlock & Woolley, the following list includes those who have worked on the most recent projects. Our gratitude and acknowledgment also go to those who represented the practice at earlier times.

Malcolm Alger
Philip Baigent
Tom Bomford
Halina Bradford
Leigh Cashel
Stephen Chan
Nick Cooney
Tom Dash
Janine Deshon
Azar Djamali
Yolanta Dyga
Paul Ferry
Janine Fowlstone
Robert Godfrey
Hany Habib
Linda Hawkins
Bindi Hooghuis
Bhathiya Jinasena
Taissa Kang
Matt Kenchington
Tina Lei
David Ma
Ameera Mahmood
Helmut Rhode
Deanne Rose
Ray Stevens
Dale Swan
Lasz Szabo
Nicholas Tesdorff
Steve Thomas
Jason Trisley
Tom Vandenberg
Lynn Vlismas
Garry Wallace
Michael Warren
Steve Warren
Priscilla Williams
Justin Wong
Robin Yeap
Gaetane Zuffery

A large number of architects who worked as assistants at Ancher Mortlock & Woolley have later gone on to establish their own practices and high reputations. Since Sydney Ancher founded it, the practice has always been run as a design directorate; that is, the principals have been responsible for the conception and the creative control of development of all the office's design work. A great contribution to the high quality of Ancher Mortlock & Woolley design has been the ability of those professionals, who, although transient, assisted in implementing the designs. Of particular significance, however, have been the efforts of the long-term colleagues, currently Directors and Associates in the firm.

Photography Credits

Leigh Atkinson: 97 (2); 98 (4,5)

Tom Balfour: 112 (1,2); 113 (3); 117 (10–13); 128 (1,3); 129 (4); 130 (6); 131 (8)

Phil Baigent: 176 (2–4); 177 (5–8); 178 (9,10); 179 (13–15)

Patrick Bingham-Hall: 168 (2); 169 (3); 171 (6,7); 172 (10,12); 173 (13); 204 (1); 205 (3,4); 206 (7); 207 (9,10); 208 (11); 210 (12–14); 213 (3); 215 (5); 217 (10,11); 218 (12)

Virginia Braden: 228

Max Dupain: 40 (2); 41 (2); 42 (1,3); 44 (1–3); 45 (4); 46 (1,2); 51 (3,4); 54 (1,2); 55 (5–7); 58 (1); 59 (3,4); 60 (7); 61 (8,9); 62 (2–5); 63 (6); 64 (1,2); 65 (5); 66 (2); 67 (4,5); 72 (5); 76 (2); 78 (1); 80 (3); 81 (6); 84 (7); 85 (8); 86 (1); 87 (3,4); 90 (6,8); 91 (9); 95 (5); 96 (1); 102 (4); 103 (6); 104 (1); 105 (7,8); 106 (1,3); 107 (4); 108 (6,8); 109 (11); 119 (4); 120 (8)

Montgomery Dunn: 42 (2)

Tim Collis-Bird: 200 (2–4)

Scott Francis: 154 (1)

Fretwell Photography: 150 (2)

John Gollings: 134 (6); 138 (1,2); 140 (3); 143 (6–8); 144 (10–12); 145 (13,14); 147 (15); 148 (2,4); 149 (5,6); 171 (8); 172 (11)

David Moore: 47 (2,3); 52 (2,3); 53 (5)

Michael Nicholson: 82 (1–3); 118 (1,3); 124 (3); 125 (4–6); 126 (8); 127 (10–14); 174 (1–3); 175 (4,5)

Eric Sierins: 132 (1–3); 133 (4); 136 (9); 137 (10); 151 (3); 152 (5); 153 (7); 154 (2); 155 (3); 157 (6,7); 158 (8,10); 159 (12); 160 (13); 161 (14); 162 (1,2); 163 (3); 164 (4); 165 (8); 180 (1–3); 182 (5,6); 183 (7); 188 (3); 189 (4); 190 (5); 191 (7,8); 192 (9–11); 194 (1,2); 196 (5,6); 198 (7); 199 (8–10); 200 (1); 201 (5); 202 (6,7); 203 (10)

Eric Sierins/Max Dupain & Associates: 181 (4); 183 (8)

Harry Sowden: 67 (3); 68 (2); 69 (6); 70 (8); 72 (1,2); 73 (4,5); 74 (6); 75 (8)

Garry Wallace: 188 (1); 207 (8)

Ken Woolley: 55 (4); 77 (4,5); 88 (2); 89 (3); 90 (7); 92 (1,4–6); 93 (1–4); 94 (2,3); 95 (4,6); 100 (2,3); 101 (4–8); 102 (1,2); 103 (7); 104 (2); 105 (4,5); 108 (7,9); 119 (5); 120 (6,7); 122 (1–4); 123 (7–10); 124 (1)

David Young: 110 (2); 111 (4–6); 121 (1,2,4)

Index

Bold page numbers refer to projects included in Selected and Current Works